Adoption in a
Color-Blind Society

Perspectives on a Multiracial America series

Joe R. Feagin, Texas A & M University, series editor

The racial composition of the United States is rapidly changing. Books in the series will explore various aspects of the coming multiracial society, one in which European-Americans are no longer the majority and where issues of white-on-black racism have been joined by many other challenges to white dominance.

Titles:

Elizabeth M. Aranda, *Emotional Bridges to Puerto Rico: Migration, Return Migration, and the Struggles of Incorporation*

Melanie Bush, *Breaking the Code of Good Intentions: Everyday Forms of Whiteness*

Victoria Kaplan, *Structural Inequality: Black Architects in the United States*

Amir Mavasti and Karyn McKinney, *Unwelcome Immigrants: Middle Eastern Lives in America*

Katheryn Russell-Brown, *Protecting Our Own: Race, Crime, and African Americans*

Forthcoming titles include:

Erica Chito Childs, *Fade to Black and White*

Richard Rees, *Shades of Difference: A History of Ethnicity in America*

Adoption in a
Color-Blind Society

PAMELA ANNE QUIROZ

ROWMAN & LITTLEFIELD PUBLISHERS, INC.
Lanham • Boulder • New York • Toronto • Plymouth, UK

ROWMAN & LITTLEFIELD PUBLISHERS, INC.

Published in the United States of America
by Rowman & Littlefield Publishers, Inc.
A wholly owned subsidiary of The Rowman & Littlefield Publishing Group, Inc.
4501 Forbes Boulevard, Suite 200, Lanham, Maryland 20706
www.rowmanlittlefield.com

Estover Road, Plymouth PL6 7PY, United Kingdom

British Library Cataloguing in Publication Information Available

Library of Congress Cataloging-in-Publication Data
Quiroz, Pamela Anne, 1960-
  Adoption in a color-blind society / Pamela Anne Quiroz.
    p. cm. — (Perspectives on a multiracial America series)
  Includes bibliographical references and index.
  ISBN-13: 978-0-7425-5941-7 (cloth : alk. paper)
  ISBN-10: 0-7425-5941-6 (cloth : alk. paper)
  ISBN-13: 978-0-7425-5942-4 (pbk. : alk. paper)
  ISBN-10: 0-7425-5942-4 (pbk. : alk. paper)
  1. Interracial adoption—United States. 2. Adoption—United States. 3. Adoption—United States—Public opinion. I. Title.
  HV875.64.Q85 2007
  362.734089'00973—dc22
                                                      2007006441

Printed in the United States of America

∞™ The paper used in this publication meets the minimum requirements of American National Standard for Information Sciences—Permanence of Paper for Printed Library Materials, ANSI/NISO Z39.48-1992.

To Tommie Lee Ragland

"The 'good fight' is living life so that the eternal qualities of God may be found in us and sought in our fellow persons; not merely as a religious exercise, but as the inner glow of every now. . . . As I seek God's eternal qualities in my fellow persons, your eternal now lights up my life as I engage in my own good fight." —TLR

Contents

Acknowledgments   xi

1 Introduction   1
    Outline of Chapters   7
    Why Private Adoption and Internet Data?   8
    Researching on the Internet   10

2 Color-Blind Racism in the United States/Color-Blind
    Individualism in Adoption   13
    Color-Blind Ideology and Racism   13
    Color-Blind Racism and Racial Inequality   16
    Color-Blind Individualism and Adoption Policy   18
    Color-Blind Individualism in the Global Market   21

3 Racial Projects and the Changing Discourse of Adoption   29
    Cultural Texts   30
    Adoption, Child Welfare, and Eugenics (1900–1960) 31
    Matching   34
    Adoption, Civil Rights, and Women's Liberation (1960–2000) 36
        Segregation, Miscegenation, and Integration 36
        Women's Liberation   37
    The "New" Adoption Discourse: Rearticulating Race? (1980–2004) 41
    The Language of Race on Private Agency Websites   46
    Conclusion   50

4 Race Practice: The Dynamics of Race in Private Adoption   55
   Data Sources   55
   Website Searches   56
   The Open Directory Project (dmoz.org)   56
   Adoption.com   59
   Changes in Patterns and Market Forces of Adoption   62
   Demand-Side Dynamics   63
   Minority Children in U.S. Private Adoption Agency Programs   67
   Nonexplicit Minority Programs   69
   Criteria for Adoption   70
   Adoption and the Latin-Americanization of Race in the
   United States   76
   International Adoption: The Alternative to Minority Programs?   77
   Conclusion   79

5 "Race Talk" in Adoption Forums   83
   Adoptive Parent Profiles   83
   Adoption Forums   86
   Adoption.com   88
       Race Chat: White Privilege   88
       Race Categories: Taboo Words, or "Why Can't We Say
       That, Too?"   91
       African American Supply and Placement   94
       Family Acceptance   94
       Color Consciousness   98
       Hair and Skin   101
       Rainbow Families   102
       Color Blindness   104
   NYSCCC.org   106
       Are We Prejudiced?   106
       Transracial Adoption by White Gay Couples   106
       Reverse Discrimination?   107
       Race as Primary Identity   109
   Conclusion   110

6 Transnational, Transracial, and Minority Adoption and
Public Policy 111
Intercountry Adoption 112
Private Domestic Adoption 116

References 119
Index 133
About the Author 141

Acknowledgments

In thirteen years as an academic I had never been motivated to write a book. I did write a prospectus and even obtained a contract for my dissertation but never began the manuscript, no doubt because my motivation at that time was pursuit of tenure and not the work itself. My first acknowledgement, therefore, should be to my son, Justin. It was my search for Justin that first stimulated the questions and later was the impetus for this book. It is also my mea culpa to Justin for being part of a system that benefits some (adoptive persons and couples) at the expense of others (birth families and their children). Regardless of how I may frame the benefits to all persons involved in adoption, there is no denying that the rhetoric serves to assuage my conscience and minimize the pain of separation to which I contribute as an adoptive parent.

Writing a book takes time. For the opportunity to focus exclusively on this process I would like to credit a UIC sabbatical and a fellowship provided by the Institute for Research on Race and Public Policy. I would also like to thank my chair Mark Smylie for his support in this effort and my colleague Steve Tozer for his advice. Particular thanks also goes to my colleague Amanda Lewis, with whom I conversed on this topic during several coffee breaks and who initially began this effort with me. Unfortunately Amanda had to remove herself due to multiple obligations and limited time. Nevertheless, she assisted me in the initial framing of the work, wrote a research article on it, and stimulated me to pursue this work as a manuscript. My debt to her is significant.

I also want to thank colleagues who have read and commented on the work in its various stages, both known (Howard Winant, Judith Blau, and of course Joe Feagin) and unknown (anonymous reviewers).

Friends and family have also supported this effort. In my goal to write an accessible book, I asked several of them to read parts of it. So thank you Agnes, Lois, Sandra, and Michele. I thank my mother for teaching me how to be a mother and providing my first experience of unconditional love, the most valuable gift one human being can give to another. My husband, Jim, has been another source of this type of love and has given generously of his time and support during this effort. I am deeply appreciative and want to thank him for this and for Justin.

Finally, much of this work was written while my dearest friend lay dying in the hospital. In fact, it was written by her bedside. She was my mentor and my heart. She opened many doors for me and taught me many things, some of which I only now understand after her death. Her life was a testament not only to how a good academic mentor and teacher can literally alter the life of a young person, but more importantly to the significance of being a kind, just, and good person. I promised her that I would complete the work. Tommie, I owe you more than I can possibly say and I shall miss you for the rest of my life.

1

Introduction

Currently in the United States, a growing shift is under way in thinking on racial matters. A new color-blind racial logic has become increasingly popular, if not dominant, in shaping the American racial imaginary (Ansell 1997; Bobo, Kluegel, and Smith 1997; Bonilla-Silva 2003; Brown et al. 2003; Brunsma 2006; Crenshaw 1997; Doane 2003; Gallagher 2003; Herring 2004; Sears, Sidanius, and Bobo 2001). Unlike the color-blind ideal expressed as part of the civil rights movement, this new color-blind discourse involves the belief that people now *are* color-blind, judging others by the "content of their character" rather than the "color of their skin." A number of indicators suggest that people generally downplay the significance of race in shaping life opportunity or in their own thinking. Underlying the claim that people no longer "see" or "notice" race (Brown et al. 2003; Williams 2003; Blum 2002; Goldberg 2002) are several guiding assumptions: (1) that the civil rights movement was successful, and therefore race no longer shapes life opportunities; (2) that with the exception of a few extremists on the margins, racism has largely disappeared; (3) that since the United States is rapidly becoming a color-blind society, there is no need for race-conscious policies such as affirmative action that provide unwarranted advantages to people of color; (4) that since the United States increasingly functions as a racial meritocracy, it is annoying, if not racially problematic, when people of color "play the race card" and try to bring race in where it doesn't belong. As the popular refrain goes, "I don't see color. Black, white, red, purple, green, it's all the same to me."

Despite these popular claims, significant evidence shows that race continues to matter in multiple ways. National survey data show that a majority of
whites believe that discrimination against racial minorities no longer exists,
that blacks have as good a chance as whites to procure housing, find a job, or
achieve middle-class status (Bobo and Kluegel 1997; Gallagher 2003; Shipler
1998). The 2000 General Social Survey found that 51 percent of whites attributed the low socioeconomic status of blacks to a lack of effort (Herring 2004).
Qualitative studies detailing the parameters of these new racial narratives have
also been collected in a number of states and regions across the country (e.g.,
Detroit, Michigan; Georgia; California; Florida; Oregon; Colorado; and the
Northeast). In studies of white college students in three different regions,
Bonilla-Silva and Forman (2000) found a predominance of color-blind thinking illustrated in part by students denying the existence of discrimination or
judging it as "isolated incidents."

These popular sentiments are echoed by prominent public figures, politicians, and academics who are proponents of this color-blind perspective.
Proposition 54 in California, intended to outlaw the collection of racial and
ethnic data in the state, gained much attention and national support before
narrowly losing in the polls. The proposition was based on the idea that race
no longer mattered and such data were superfluous if not actually problematic.
Proponents such as Ward Connerly, a national leader in the effort to dismantle
affirmative action, argued that the collection of such data was actually responsible for perpetuating the focus on race. Similarly, scholars and pundits from
Abigail and Stephen Thernstrom to Dinesh D'Souza have hailed the end of
racism and argue that the solution to our racial problems (as they define them)
is to get rid of race-conscious policies and end our national fixation on race
(D'Souza 1995; Thernstrom and Thernstrom 1999; Jacoby 1998; Sleeper 1997).

Part of the larger context of these color-blind claims is the real and important victories of the civil rights movement. Explicit racism in arenas such as
housing or hiring has been outlawed. In daily practice it is socially unaccept-
able to express racist sentiments in public places. But asserting that discrimination is no longer a factor in American life takes the ideal of "freedom from
discrimination" and presumes it to be an achieved reality. The common claim
that people no longer see color, that it is really a nonissue, contradicts other
social patterns. A growing body of research indicates that new laws making
discrimination illegal have not, in fact, meant the end of pervasive discrimi-

nation. This work shows that race is still a part of everyday interactions, housing, and hiring processes, just in more subtle and covert ways than in the past (Shapiro 2004). Race is also a salient issue in important life choices such as where one buys a home, where one sends a child to school, and who one takes as a life partner (Johnson and Shapiro 2003; Krysan 2002a, 2002b; Farley et al. 1994; Lewis 2001; Massey and Fisher 1999; Yinger, 1995).

Echoing this larger push toward color blindness in racial discourse has been a substantial shift in policy making in specific arenas. One such arena is adoption. Nowhere is America's schism with regard to race more evident than in the field of adoption. The role of race in adoption and public policy on adoption began shifting in the 1970s and culminated in the Multi-Ethnic Placement and Inter-Ethnic Placement Acts, both passed in the mid-1990s. These laws prohibit denying or delaying adoption placement based on race, reversing the traditional stance taken by adoption professionals in the context of a historically color-conscious society, with its political and legal sanctions against race mixing. Several contrasting ideas about the role of race in adoption coexisted in the decades before these laws were passed. The first, supported by several constituencies, the National Association of Black Social Workers and black activists among others, actively opposed transracial adoption by arguing that maintaining the racial integrity of adoptive families was imperative to providing appropriate racial socialization and maintaining communities. At the center of their argument was a presumption that racism is a permanent feature of our society that will inevitably shape the life experiences of black children. Some of these advocates viewed transracial adoption as racial and cultural genocide; others argued that the principles of color-blind individualism undergirding calls for transracial adoption were nothing more than convenient posturing to satisfy the demand of white adoptive parents by providing them with access to the children of minority populations (Perry 1998).

A second perspective, represented by "color-blind" individualists during the 1980s and 1990s, argued that racism could be eradicated by absorbing minority children into families who may or may not be of similar racial background (through transracial and international adoption) and that primacy should be given to family-building over the maintenance of communities or racial/ethnic groups (Bartholet 1991; Mahoney 1991). These groups contended that family-building by adoptive parents should occur without

interference from either the state or the child's community of origin. Advocates of this perspective have spoken of the best interests of black children and
specifically of rescuing them from languishing in the foster care system. Color
blindness in the adoption process, they said, would be good for everyone, and
those who try to argue against it were bringing race in where it did not belong
(Logan n.d.; McRoy 1989; Perry 1994; Vieni 1975).[1]

The legal maneuverings that led to the passage of the Multi-Ethnic Placement Act and the Inter-Ethnic Placement Act represented the triumph of
color-blind individualists and elevated the rights of white adoptive parents
over those of birth parents and their children. Transracial adoption, related
international adoption practices, and the rhetoric surrounding these practices
seem to be consistent with the notions and values of a color-blind society. Related to the logic of color-blind thinking, these adoption policy changes and
the defense of them are based on the assumptions that race is no longer relevant and that if liberal activists and government officials would just get out of
the way, it would be possible for race consciousness to fade away and for adoption to provide one means of eradicating the fixation on race and racism. The
problem with the color-blind perspective (and even, in some ways, with the
group-consciousness perspective) is the assumption that whites are eagerly
waiting to adopt infants and children of color; that there is a significant demand for transracial adoption (typically defined by private adoption agencies
to mean African American and biracial infants); and that people are, in fact,
already color-blind. Although African American infants and children *are* being adopted in larger numbers, there is not a significantly greater demand for
African American infants and children compared with the demand for infants
of other racial/ethnic groups (Courtney 1997; Freundlich 2000a; Roberts
2002). In addition, several private U.S. adoption agencies now look to Cana-
dian and European couples to place African American and biracial infants because of the lack of demand for these children (ABC World News 2005; NAIC
2004b). As Banks (1998) outlines, there is a persistent preference for white infants among white adoptive parents, who are also the majority of adoptive
parents: "Adoptive parents' racial preferences dramatically diminish the pool
of potential parents available to black children relative to that available to
white children" (p. 2). Thus, the reality of adoption practices, particularly in
private arrangements, seems to stand in stark contrast to color-blind rhetoric
and adoption policies.

Adoption structures not only seem to lay bare the lie of color-blind discourse but also reveal that rather than eroding, the meaning of race is shifting. The particular way in which infants of color are categorized within the adoption world in many ways bridges the old with the new—what some are calling the Latin-Americanization of race in the United States. Three-tiered adoption pricing schemes and the particular way biracial children are either "downgraded" or "upgraded" depending on their heritage illustrates well what Bonilla-Silva (2003) and Bonilla-Silva and Glover (2004) have described as a tri-racial, Latin American–like system emerging in the United States in which whites remain at the top while an intermediary group of "honorary whites" serves as a buffer between whites and blacks. That is, new racial arrangements seem to include at least three categories—those who are labeled white, honorary white, and collective black.

Using the term *Latin American–like* because of the system's similarity to the more complicated racial landscapes of Latin American countries, this thesis suggests that a growing middle category—consisting of many Asian groups, many light-skinned Latinos, and biracial persons—will function as a buffer to racial conflict between whites and the "collective black" groups. There is already ample evidence that such a middle category has begun to emerge. For example, certain Asian Americans and Latino ethnic groups have much higher intermarriage rates with whites and much lower levels of residential segregation from whites. Qualitative evidence shows that whites hold much less racial animosity toward some Asian Americans and Latinos than toward blacks (Emerson, Yancey, and Chai 2001; Taylor 1998; Wilson 1996). While Asian Americans and Latinos continue to face discrimination in some sectors, they occupy a quite distinct place in the racial imaginary. Others have argued that we are moving to a new divide in which the salient categories are black and nonblack (Yancey 2003, 2006). In either case, these new categories reflect the changing meaning of *race* in the context of shifting politics and demographics.

In the private adoption market, there is a clear pattern along comparable lines in which babies are valued both economically and emotionally at least in part according to their racial/ethnic heritage. The racial heritage of some seems to confer upon them "honorary white" status while others are categorized as nonwhite and valued less. In both domestic and international adoption practices, when white preferences must be moderated because white children are unavailable, children from Asia, Latin America, or the former

Soviet Republics often fulfill the parenting dreams of white couples. Citing the transformation of racial thinking in the United States does not mean that historic binaries based on the "one-drop" rule (Davis 1991) have entirely disappeared. Rather, we have a complicated process in which the very meaning of *biracial* varies depending on the specific heritages being mixed, mirroring what some have labeled a "pigmentocracy," the ranking of groups based upon phenotype and cultural characteristics (see Hunter 2005). Market forces and the costs of adopting different children highlight this differential valuing in a particularly dramatic fashion.

This book explores these seemingly contradictory trends through the current dynamics of race in private infant adoption, long regarded the group of children in greatest demand by adoptive parents. I argue for a less sentimental and altruistic interpretation of the new laws and policies governing adoption. Instead, adoption should be viewed more as a business, driven by market forces. Rather than moving toward a color-blind democracy nationally or globally, we instead live in a context in which race continues to matter substantially, particularly in arenas like adoption. *Adoption in a Color-Blind Society* illustrates how the political economy of private domestic adoption intersects with the political economy of racism to generate quite different demands for infants and children of different races and how the private adoption arena responds to these demands. At a time when the adoption industry has modified its position regarding birth mothers (once treated with something just short of disdain) and when we are being told that we now live in a color-blind society, it is ironic to find the general and abstract language of adoption so changed, yet the racial/ethnic distinctions in private adoptions so fixed. In the past, adoptive parents were ennobled by their willingness to take on the illegitimate and undeserving child. With the reduction of white birthrates and available white infants, the current political climate around abortion, and the market demand for white infants, the industry has reconstructed the adoption process to one that is now promoted as a "benefit" for adoptive parents.

Adoption in a Color-Blind Society provides a critical interpretation of the discursive practices of private adoption, particularly as these practices relate to race. Adoption practices can be understood as part of what Omi and Winant (1994) called "racial projects," the sociohistorical processes involved in explaining, organizing, and distributing resources according to racial categories. Racial projects have found their way into the adoption arena affecting children of color, particularly African American children. Private adoption practices provide a window into the shifting dynamics of race in the United States demonstrating that rather moving towards a color-blind democracy, we instead live in a context where race continues to matter substantially, particularly in arenas "closest to home." Moreover, examining such practices illuminates the depth of globalization and the role of U.S. citizens as "consumers" in a world marketplace that includes not just retail products and services but also human lives.

OUTLINE OF CHAPTERS

Chapter 2 presents an in-depth discussion of color-blind discourse and neo-liberal racism that have emerged in recent years, the logic of this discourse, and a review of empirical evidence supporting the pervasiveness of color-blind thinking in contemporary society. The chapter also highlights research showing that with regard to a number of important life choices, race is still quite salient. Parallel trends in adoption are mapped, including the shift in policy making in adoption and its version of color blindness, "color-blind individualism."

Chapter 3 traces how changes in the larger society have found their way into the adoption arena, resulting in new laws, policies, and participants in the adoption process and altering the discourse of adoption. An interpretive analysis of popular adoption literature and academic research, social movements, and information in the public domain provide a framework for understanding how the practices of twentieth-century adoption were part of the larger process of racial formation in the United States

Chapter 4 relies on an analysis of web-page data of private adoption agencies to describe the parameters of private adoption practice today. The complicated choices adoptive parents face as well as the ways in which these choices determine the adoptive circumstances of U.S. minority children, particularly African Americans, are presented. Web-page searches of two online directories (one with 274 and the other with 1,552 agencies) listing agencies in different regions of the country allowed me to observe the practices, price range, and policies of a significant number of agencies. The discourse on race in these websites is also examined and shows how race continues to matter to all participants in the adoption process.

Chapter 5 offers additional evidence of the continuing salience of race as a factor motivating persons/couples considering adoption by including two analyses. Two major websites of adoptive parent profiles were examined at three points in time from 2003–2005. Online profiles of adoptive parents illustrate the demand side of the adoption equation, with adoptive singles/couples across the United States stating their preferences for children by race, ethnicity, and a host of other specifications. An online observational study of two adoptive (and prospective) parent chat rooms focuses on discussions involving race and ethnicity.

Chapter 6 summarizes and identifies issues that need further debate and exploration. Theoretical, substantive, and policy issues in private adoption are discussed to illustrate how racial thinking is shifting but retaining certain key aspects of racial hierarchy, both of which continue to influence life outcomes. The imbalance between a steady demand and the decrease in supply of white infants has contributed not only to the rising costs of adoption but also the interest in looking elsewhere for newborns and toddlers (i.e., international adoption). The chapter offers a view into the racialized aspects of globalization, its effects on particular groups, and how this intersects with private infant adoption. The proliferation of private and independent adoptions contributes not only to the political economy and reconfiguring of race in the United States but also to the economies of countries abroad. Particular emphasis is given to domestic policy changes needed to regulate the private adoption industry in order to ensure the welfare of children. A call is made for greater accountability of countries and for the gathering of data on the well-being of children all over the world.

Adoption in a Color-Blind Society is intended to further discussions about racial dynamics in the United States today, as well as discussions about private adoption practices, racial inequality, social justice, and family life.

WHY PRIVATE ADOPTION AND INTERNET DATA?

Over the past two decades, private adoptions have declined from 77 percent (of all adoptions) in 1992 to 46 percent in 2001 (U.S. Department of Health and Human Services 2004). One may reasonably ask, Why then choose private adoption as the focus of a study? Private adoptions still comprise a significant segment of the adoption market, and though "intercountry," or international, adoptions are reported in separate categories by government and private adoption organizations, a substantial number of these adoptions are processed through private agencies (Freundlich 2000a; see also chapter 4, this volume).[2] If it were possible to assess the number of international adoptions facilitated by private agencies, private adoptions would likely represent over half of all adoptions.

Although private adoptions include independent, kinship, and tribal placements of infants and children, my focus is exclusively on the placement of infants and newborns into nonkinship families through for-profit and not-for-profit agencies. Along with a steady demand for infants over the past twenty years and an increase in intercountry (also known as transnational) adoptions (more than tripling from 6,472 in 1992 to 22,728 in 2005), a substantial number of children, largely African American and biracial, remain in need of adoptive homes (ACF 2005). At the same time, there has been a tremendous increase in the number of foster children (from 280,000 in 1986 to 483,000 in 1995), necessitating special laws and efforts to increase adoption of these children (Bartholet 1999; Wulczyn, Hislop, and Chen 2005). One way to understand the dilemmas of the public system is to explore the forces governing private adoption.

Private adoption remains one of the few unregulated industries in the United States, with serious implications for child welfare. States set the legal parameters for adoption expenses; however, they are not required to report the number of private and independent domestic adoptions that cost anywhere from $4,000 to more than $40,000, and the courts rarely question fees (Watson as cited in Freundlich, 2000a). To many critics private-agency infant (and intercountry) adoption has become a business in the United States; one in which supply is outstripped by demand, and where children, particularly infants, have become a commodity. The political economies of race and class are reflected in the dynamic between white middle-class adoptive parents and birth mothers, who are increasingly likely to be women of color and who are typically poor, whether the adoption is domestic or international.

Finally, private adoption is emblematic of our neoliberal democracy in which everything, including infants and children, is available in the global marketplace. Under the pretext of family rights and parental freedom of choice juxtaposed with the benefits to orphans, the market freedoms enjoyed by participants in private adoption negate issues of ethics and social responsibility and displace notions of economic, sexual, racial, and social justice.

RESEARCHING ON THE INTERNET

No single agency is responsible for collecting adoption data; therefore information must be gathered from a number of sources, including the National Center for State Courts (which collects data for the total number of adoptions processed through courts), the federal Adoption and Foster Care Analysis and Reporting System (AFCARS), the State Department, and the Office of Immigration Statistics. Because the data reflect public and intercountry adoptions, estimates of private adoptions are acquired by subtracting AFCARS and intercountry adoptions from the total adoptions reported by U.S. courts. The court system may include adoptions in a larger category (i.e., "other civil petitions") and adoptive parents may not file intercountry adoptions in the U.S. court system, reducing the accuracy of adoption reporting. The National Adoption Information Clearinghouse (NAIC) says that most private adoption agencies do not report data either on the number of children adopted through their agencies or the characteristics of the children or their adoptive and birth parents (NAIC 2004b). In an effort to gather information from a sample of these agencies, the NAIC contacted more than two hundred private agencies for information, with no agency "able or willing" to produce either adoption statistics or data about private adoptions.

My own adoption journey was also a factor in the decision to conduct an Internet-based study. When my partner and I were told by a Chicago agency that locating a Latino infant would be a difficult and protracted process, I turned to the Internet for information. It became apparent that even though all children deserved loving homes (what most private agency websites proclaimed), some children were clearly preferred over others. Those less valued in the adoption market were placed in separate adoption programs, often with a statement emphasizing the need for adoptive families in this program, and advertised with different adoption requirements and costs.

A vast amount of information is now available on the Internet, making it a valuable resource for understanding human behavior and relationships. In addition to easy access to government publications and social science statistics (e.g., U.S. Census or State Department), websites are a relatively untapped source of adoption information and alternative measures of color blindness or the lack thereof. Adoption websites are an open laboratory for content and discourse analyses of private agency data, adoptive parent profiles, and archived chat-room exchanges involving race.

Private adoption agencies use the Internet in addition to newspaper, telephone, and local advertising to advertise their services and to solicit birth mothers and adoptive parents, with each agency's representation of what they do and how they do it. The Internet is also a means of looking at large numbers of private agencies across the country. Consequently, research that would not be possible due to funding or time constraints can be done via the Internet. Like other organizations that use the Internet to advertise, private adoption agencies are likely to use websites to present themselves in the best possible light (Ó Dochartaigh 2002). Social acceptability leads agencies to downplay the extent or existence of race-based practices (e.g., by burying information on websites); therefore an analysis of websites is likely to underestimate rather than overestimate the number and extent of minority programs.

Another positive aspect of Internet research is access to archived data such as the chat-room discussions included in the book, which presents opportunities for conducting unobtrusive studies, potentially minimizing observer bias and the effects of researcher presence on interaction (Bordia 1996; Hine 2000). The intertextuality of the Internet lends itself to discourse analysis as it allows users to move seamlessly from one text to another as texts are interconnected.

Like all social science research, Internet-based studies also have limitations. For example, we cannot know whether adoptive parents who communicate on the Internet are representative of the larger adoptive parent population. This is a real problem that cannot be easily resolved; however, prior assessments of the population of Internet users suggest a correlation between adoptive parents in chat rooms and the larger adoptive parent population captured in traditional social science surveys: predominantly white, well-educated, and middle- to upper-middle class.[3]

Like private adoption, the Internet is a largely unregulated environment offering the opportunity to examine public expression without violating anonymity. My hope is that the liberating effects of cyberspace encourage greater candor, yet I recognize that anonymity also allows people to try on different identities without the checks of face-to-face interaction. The dynamic nature of the Internet is both a positive and a negative, where the flow of information on adoption can provide positive outcomes not only for persons looking to place children or adopt but also for researchers and the general public. However, websites change, making it difficult (if not impossible) to keep up with the information explosion and even more difficult to replicate research as sites are modified or disappear altogether. Equally important, information placed on the Web may be, at best, misleading and, at worst, inaccurate. In this reality added precautions and record keeping are critical (e.g., making hard-copy printouts or saving computer files). Having written this book using data gathered from the Internet, obviously I agree with those who believe that opportunities and insights such data provide outweigh the limitations. Attempts to address these limitations are made in each chapter in which Internet data is used; however, the reader must ultimately be the judge of whether the book provides a persuasive argument.

NOTES

1. Transracial adoption is neither endorsed nor condemned here as I am less interested in whether, how, and who should be adopting than in how the adoption industry represents itself and whether its discourse matches its practices. My interest is in how these practices match or contradict dominant racial discourses more generally. For those who are interested in the ethics of transracial adoption, there is abundant popular and research literature contesting the relative merits and drawbacks of such practices.

2. The terms *intercountry* and *international* are alternately used in this book.

3. The exception to this is the majority of demographic assessments of Internet users that cite males as predominant. However, the selective group of adoptive parent Internet users in the chat rooms I observed suggests a predominantly female population.

2

Color-Blind Racism in the United States/Color-Blind Individualism in Adoption

Color-blind ideology and neoliberal public policy illustrate the pervasiveness of color-blind thinking in our society. *Color-blind individualism* (Perry 1994), the adoption arena's version of color-blind discourse, is accompanied by shifts in adoption policy that promote transracial and intercountry (transnational) adoption as solutions to poverty and family disruption. These practices are supported by legislation that for the first time in adoption history outlaws consideration of race in adoption placement. Offering evidence that contradicts color-blind ideology and reveals the persistence of color consciousness in America, this chapter maps parallel trends in the adoption arena and argues that adoption, particularly private adoption, is anything but color-blind. More importantly, color-blind racism is not limited to the United States but has now become part of the new global reality.

COLOR-BLIND IDEOLOGY AND RACISM

Several contemporary discourses on race compete with one another, but one has captured the attention of politicians, scholars, and the general public: color-blind ideology. Color-blind ideology relies on race-neutral language to support the argument that race is no longer a factor in opportunity and achievement in America. This idea and the processes that promote racial inequality have also been referred to as laissez-faire (Bobo, Kluegel and Smith 1997), symbolic (Sears 1988), and neoliberal racism (Giroux 2006). Underlying assumptions common to these terms are (1) racism is a thing of the past;

(2) current achievement is based on merit and character; and (3) race-conscious policies are no longer needed and are therefore discriminatory. The general response to questions about the relationship between race and achievement is that racism in America is an artifact of the past. In a Gallup survey conducted in 2001, seven of ten whites said that blacks were treated the same as whites. Another study on race and ethnicity found 71 percent of whites believed that African Americans have either the same or "more" opportunities than whites (Kaiser Foundation 2001). Part of this argument resides in the dismantling of legal segregation and changing white attitudes toward African Americans. Political and cultural hegemony also allows the racial order to be defined by whites and at the same time renders white privilege invisible (Feagin 2003; McIntosh 1989). Highlighting the invisibility of white privilege, a study of 246 working- and middle-class men and women born in the United States found that whites believe we now live in a meritocracy in which a person's success is the consequence of qualifications and proper characteristics (hard work, ambition, and ability) (DiTomaso, Parks-Yancy, and Post 2003). Even though the majority of study participants obtained jobs through their social capital (networks of family, friends, and acquaintances), whites minimized the significance of networks and economic resources they were able to access. By minimizing the influence of their social networks and claiming an ethic of fairness and merit, the belief that race was unimportant in life opportunities was reinforced and participants were also able to deny their role in reproducing inequalities. These attitudes represent what Bonilla-Silva (2001) calls "white-habitus," the ability of whites to maintain a socially and consciously constructed all-white environment in which they live their everyday lives. Color-blind logic privatizes the discourse on race by defining racial problems as private ones, thus allowing whites to maintain individualistic interpretations of racial inequality.

White racial attitudes have been accompanied by white opposition to public policies designed to achieve racial equality (Bobo 2004; Sears 1988). The claim of color blindness belies an awareness of whiteness that emerges whenever the dominant group's position is threatened (Ebert 2004). Recent examples include the border-patrolling right-wing vigilante group the Minutemen and the proposed Sensenbrenner bill (HR 4437), which criminalizes persons gaining illegal entry to the United States. Both examples are indicative of chauvinistic and racist positions that align with nationalism and whiteness whenever significant increases in immigration occur. Unlike those who suggest that whites maintain "sincere fictions" regarding racism and their role in perpetuating it (Feagin and Vera 1995; DiTomaso, Parks-Yancy and Post 2003), Henry Giroux argues for an interpretation of greater culpability over one of benign neglect and suggests that color blindness "offers up a highly racialized understanding of racial inequality (though paraded as transcendent) notion of agency, while also providing an ideological space free of guilt, self-reflection, and political responsibility, despite the fact that blacks have a disadvantage in almost all areas of social life: housing, jobs, education, income levels, mortgage lending and basic everyday services" (2006, 77).

Giroux is not the only one to question the sincerity of color-blind advocates. In *Freedom Is Not Enough* (2006), a provocative look at the role of the workforce in the struggle for equality, historian Nancy MacLean argues how a movement led by conservative politicians, academics, and activists cultivated color-blind racism and the invisibility of white privilege in order to reverse the accomplishments of the civil rights movement. A conscious backlash against the potential loss of white privilege, color-blind racism is less naive and altruistic than instrumental.

> By the 1970s, the thrust would shift from claims that (white) ethnics also faced bias to the assertion that blacks held a "privileged" position. . . . In fact, white ethnic Americans' greatest progress had come as a result of the New Deal, with its two-track social policies that disadvantaged most blacks and Latinos and its mortgage backing for segregated housing in red-lined communities, which enabled even wage-earning whites to amass capital to which people of color were denied access, as well as the later GI Bill, whose education benefits favored whites disproportionately because so many Jim Crow colleges lacked accreditation. (MacLean 2006, 245)

Common conceptions of achievement by race also relate media presentations of African Americans in various roles with the fallacy that images of achievement reflect realities lived. Though it is true that "biological" racism and legal forms of discrimination have substantially diminished and African Americans and whites now interact frequently, the stereotypes and beliefs whites have about African Americans remain inexorably tied to race (Hudson and Hines-Hudson 1999; Bobo 2004; Schuman et al. 1997; Brown et al. 2004; Hunt 2001; Hunt et al. 2000). More importantly, enduring racial antagonisms maintain the racialized system of the United States. Though many white Americans reject racial injustice, they also do not believe it occurs anymore. Those who do believe racial inequities persist are not inclined to support measures that would alleviate the inequities. Instead, their positioning on policies involving equity implies that "persons of color have many sympathizers, but few real allies" (Hudson and Hines-Hudson 1999). In this way, white supremacy continues to be sustained even when race categories are redefined.

The paradox of race is that the discourse on race and racism has changed substantially, but the material reality of race has not. Much of the debate surrounding the construct of race (some argue it is shifting and others claim it is now immaterial) revolves around efforts to redefine or eliminate racial categories without substantively altering the lived realities of persons of color. Attitudes are linked to behaviors with the assumption that the way people present themselves in surveys and interviews is consonant with what they actually do. A sizeable body of literature indicates that America may "talk the talk" but continues not to "walk the walk."

COLOR-BLIND RACISM AND RACIAL INEQUALITY

During the 1990s, when color-blind logic began to dominate and race-conscious policies were being dismantled, other events were also occurring that underscored the centrality of race (see table 2.1).

These events do not include the growth of racial/ethnic conflicts on university campuses, charges of racial profiling against police, or legal challenges to affirmative action such as the claim of reverse discrimination. Several incidents were accompanied by opinion polls conducted at the time that made the racial divide transparent. More recent events also serve as reminders of how race and ethnicity continue to pervade not only our imaginations but also our policy: a growing immigrant population has provided the impetus for immigration reform and prompted Congress to declare English the national language.

In *Whitewashing Race* (2003), Brown and colleagues challenge color-blind ideology and offer interpretations regarding the significant disparities between African Americans and whites in every area of social life. Whether the issue is access to quality education, health care, and housing; the criminal justice system; or wealth, *Whitewashing Race* illustrates the continuing effects of race on life opportunities in America. At the beginning of the twenty-first century, over half of all black families are below the poverty line and black

Table 2.1.

1991	The U.S. Senate Judiciary Committee investigated Supreme Court nominee Clarence Thomas, accused of sexual harassment by professor Anita Hill, in the first confirmation hearing to be televised nationally.
1991	A videotape of Rodney King being beaten by four white policemen as Mr. King exhibited no resistance to arrest was highly publicized.
1991	Race riots in South Central Los Angeles followed a "not guilty" verdict for policemen involved in the arrest and beating of Rodney King.
1993	The U.S. Justice Department sued Denny's restaurant chain for discrimination against African American customers.
1994	Susan Smith, a white mother who drowned her two sons, lied on national television, stating that a black man kidnapped the children, before confessing to the crimes.
1995	O. J. Simpson was accused and tried for the murders of Nicole Brown Simpson and Ronald Goldman.
1995	Members of the Ku Klux Klan poured flammable liquids on the floor of a one-hundred-year-old black Baptist church, completely destroying it. (This was one of several rural black churches burned in the mid-1990s.)
1996	The Oakland, California, School Board officially recognized Black English (Ebonics), setting off a controversy among scholars, educators, and the general public.
1996	U.S. Justice Department data reported more than 5,000 hate crimes based on race (61 percent of all hate crimes), with the majority of these crimes committed against African Americans.
1997	Four New York City police officers assaulted a Haitian immigrant who was in custody. One of the officers sodomized Abner Louima with a toilet plunger.
1998	Three men associated with the Texas Ku Klux Klan dragged a black man (James Byrd Jr.) to his death.

poverty rates are over twice that of whites. Black morbidity and mortality rates are also significantly higher than whites', with African Americans at greater risk for diseases such as asthma and diabetes and more likely to die from cancer and heart disease. African Americans are also the most residentially segregated group in the United States and, therefore, the most educationally segregated (Massey and Denton 1993; Patillo-McCoy 1999; Lewis et al. 2004; Orfield and Eaton 1997; Orfield and Ashkinaze 1991; Boger and Orfield 2006; Kozol 2005). Given these realities and the correlations between place of residence, quality of education, and participation in the labor market, it is not surprising that income and wealth disparities between blacks and whites are also significant. Whether the focus is employment, occupation, wages, or wealth, African Americans are always at the bottom of the economic ladder (Conley 1999; Oliver and Shapiro 1997; Shapiro 2004).

According to proponents of color-blind discourse, segregation reflects black preferences rather than housing discrimination; health care issues and mortality rates reflect poor lifestyle choices of African Americans rather than asymmetric power relations between racial groups and poorer health care provided to blacks; poverty and disparities in wealth reflect lack of responsibility and effort on the part of African Americans rather than educational and labor market discrimination. Half a decade after *Brown v. Board of Education*, Anthony Platt (1997, 47) reminds us that it is still the reality that most people of color in the United States "on a daily basis, think twice about how they can best survive the day without experiencing paternalism, insults, or much, much worse."

COLOR-BLIND INDIVIDUALISM AND ADOPTION POLICY

The degree to which America is color-blind is evident in yet another institution, the child welfare system. The number of black children in foster care doubled to over 40 percent of the total foster care population between 1982 and 1999, even though black children represented only 17 percent of the nation's youth (U.S. Department of Health and Human Services 2000). In *Shattered Bonds* (2002), Dorothy Roberts reveals the U.S. foster care system for what it is: a racist system where families are monitored, regulated, and punished for being poor and black. Roberts insists the racist history of child welfare described in *Children of the Storm* (Billingsley and Giovannoni 1972) continues as color-blind ideology drives child welfare policies that undermine if not literally destroy African American families.

Color-blind individualism supports new policies that govern the foster care system and encourage severing biological family ties in favor of immediate adoption of children. Advocates of color-blind individualism maintain that race should not matter in adoption; racism can be eradicated through transracial adoption; and individual rights should be exercised without the interference of the state (Bartholet 1991; Kennedy 2003; Mahoney 1991). The logic of color-blind individualism has even greater currency in private adoption. Individual agency, a component of color-blind ideology, is critical to participants in private and independent adoption, and in the 1990s Congress passed laws to support color-blind adoption practice. Reflecting the desires of the dominant culture and certainly adoptive parents (also dominantly white), the Multi-Ethnic and Inter-Ethnic Placement Acts of 1994 and 1996 denied consideration of race in adoption placement and shifted adoption from a utilitarian function to familial entitlement. Like the upside-down world of Lewis

Carroll's *Through the Looking Glass*, racism was turned on its head as those who argued against the laws (the National Association of Black Social Workers, activists, and academics) were accused of being racist and indifferent to the best interests of black children.

Little attention is given by color-blind individualists to the traditionally discriminatory practices of the child welfare system. Instead, color-blind individualists look to transracial and minority adoption as the solutions. Absorbing African American children into a white hegemonic system is promoted as race-neutral, altruistic, and advantageous to children of color. Appropriate to a consumer-oriented society, private adoption presents adopting children of color (or not adopting them) as a matter of individual taste and lifestyle. The sanctions of law support this practice, in which individuals celebrate market freedoms without having to address considerations of community interests or equity.

Though current adoption policy is driven by the broader neoliberal perspective, in which family formation is freed from state intervention and race is mandated as irrelevant (unless, of course, it is relevant to the adopting couple), race and class privilege become transparent in private adoption. In the U.S. child welfare system, African American families are disproportionately stripped of their rights, and their children are placed in foster care or adopted (Roberts 2002; Brown et al. 2003). In private adoption, when birth mothers voluntarily place their children for adoption, African American children are separated into race-based programs, marketed, and valued in accordance with social constructions that remain embedded in a racial hierarchy. As chapters 3 and 4 illustrate, regardless of whether African American birth mothers working with private agencies give birth to perfectly healthy children, the language used to describe children in these programs reflects the common perception that something is wrong with them. Guarantees are even made by some agencies about the health status of African American and biracial children. Widely held and generally negative dispositions toward blacks (i.e., "the market") work in tandem with adoption language to generate public presentations of African American infants and children as expendable commodities that one can obtain easily and purchase cheap.

Stereotypes of African American infants and children as drug dependent, suffering from fetal alcohol syndrome or pediatric AIDS, seem to have less salience when applied to white children in other countries (Ukraine, Russia, and Romania). In the National Adoption Attitudes Survey (Harris Interactive 2002), 50 percent of participants believed that international adoption is easier than domestic adoption; however, nearly half also believed that children adopted from other countries are more likely to have "significant" medical or emotional problems. Nevertheless, international adoptions have increased substantially, particularly from certain countries. British demographer and intercountry adoption expert Peter Selman points to "the picture emerging in the United States with numbers doubling in the last five years—suggests that there is a growing demand for young light-skinned healthy babies, which has led to a trade in children from and to countries" (2001, 23).

The difficulty of demonstrating racism is the same in private adoption as in other social contexts. When racism is defined to mean intentional individual prejudice, it becomes nearly impossible to determine racist practice in private adoption. As reviewers of a journal submission pointed out, couples are not racist when they do not wish to adopt African American infants and children; rather, they are opting for similarity in family phenotype, cognizant of and responsive to the sentiments of African Americans who oppose transracial adoption, or merely feel inadequate to offer the appropriate socialization for black or biracial children. Furthermore, adoption agencies are not discriminating by placing African American and biracial children into race-based adoption programs and marketing those programs using different criteria. Rather, agencies endeavor to place needy children into families by whatever means possible, and if that requires reduced fees, increased age requirements, an open or flexible family structure and lifestyle, so be it. An argument made by one reviewer stated that the only way to truly demonstrate whether or not adoption agencies are color-blind is to ask them. To critique an argument of color-blind racism, the focus is on the motivations of white couples and private agencies.

In short, if racism is defined as antiblack sentiment, it is virtually impossible to provide evidence when even "whiteness studies" researchers typically fail to elicit overt prejudice in interviews (though surveys done by the National Opinion Research Center–University of Chicago have found such attitudes). However, if racism is examined as a system that privileges and reproduces the dominance of whiteness, then we can surely regard private adoption in America as color conscious. To paraphrase and apply Catherine McKinnon's (1989) explanation of sex discrimination to race, the dominant white culture implicitly defines the standards it claims to neutrally apply to persons of color. White perspectives define quality in scholarship, white experiences define merit, whites' postimmigrant generational status and countries of origin define who is worthy of citizenship, white history defines history. These are the standards that are defined as color-blind and ignore the power of whites to produce and reproduce racial reality. American institutions clearly remain color conscious, and as Brown and colleagues (2003) point out, the color is white.

It is no accident that African Americans have traditionally engaged in informal adoption, and have been reluctant to utilize the formal mechanisms of adoption. It should be no surprise that the legacy of slavery, Jim Crow statutes, and current discrimination practices leave African Americans less able to participate in private adoption practices that can be costly. In our current color-blind myopia, the lack of African American families available to adopt African American children is presented as a puzzle to be solved with appropriate advertising to black families. At the same time, the force of the law is in place to support the rights of white families to adopt children of the African American community. Even more problematic, color-blind racism is not limited to the United States but is now part of the new global reality.

COLOR-BLIND INDIVIDUALISM IN THE GLOBAL MARKET

In our postdemocratic era, where the market is the solution to all problems and issues of social responsibility are considered passé, Guillermo Gómez-Peña (2003) raises a number of questions: "Why are Western policies increasingly isolationist and xenophobic? Why do neoliberals want to criminalize immigrants yet advocate open borders from north to south? Why are the homeless living in the streets?" To these I would add questions about adoption: Why are some children valued and others are not? Why is intercountry adoption promoted for some U.S.-born children and not for others? Why has it taken the United States so long to ratify the Hague Convention Treaty (an internationally developed framework that calls for monitoring intercountry adoptions)?

One of the many ironies of globalization is how societies have been brought closer together through technology and transportation, yet inequalities within and between societies have been exacerbated as national, political, and cultural statuses are disrupted, identities redefined, and measures for exclusion redrawn (Sklair 2004; Weiss 2006). There are those who argue that racism goes hand in hand with globalization to delimit the participants in the market. Andrew Barlow (2003) explains a nation's racial response to globalization as the result of a number of factors, including position within the international order, history of racism, extent of migration, and oppressed groups' ability to resist racism. It is within Barlow's framework that private and intercountry adoption can be situated. Because a substantial number of intercountry adoptions by U.S. citizens are facilitated by private agencies, the terms *private/intercountry* and *transnational* are used.

Free trade now includes human trade in the form of transnational labor, mail-order brides, sex workers, and child commerce (child migrants and laborers, sex workers, and intercountry adoptees) (Ehrenreich and Hoschschild 2002). In the new global reality, infants and children are commodified and commercialized, and like most transnational migrants, adoptees in the "diaper diaspora" typically move from poor countries to wealthy ones (Selman 2001).[1] Comprising less than 5 percent of the migrating population to the United States, transnational adoptees have not been a significant factor in national population growth (Tarmann 2007). However, attendant to privatization and precipitating demographic and cultural factors, U.S. participation in transnational adoptions has grown from 6,472 in 1992 to 22,728 in 2005. Reasons for the increased number of children from sending countries involved in intercountry adoption include poverty, lack of contraception, proscriptions against birth outside of marriage, social and economic collapse (particularly in postcommunist countries), and preferences for male children (e.g., the one-child rule in China, the world's largest "sending" country in adoption; Masson 2001). However, given added complexities of crossing international borders, paperwork, institutionalization, unknown health factors, and limited information, several researchers have attempted to understand the increase in this activity by adoptive parents.

An early view framed adoption practices as altruistic attempts to absorb children who were victims of war, famine, and/or disease, with an assumption that when circumstances changed and needs diminished, so, too, would transnational adoptions (Simon and Alstein 1991). A more recent and critical argument associates intercountry adoption with prevailing (though unstated) prejudices of U.S. and European couples resistant to open adoption. In this argument national citizenship and the Western philosophy of personal identity, proprietorship, and property conflicts with the philosophy of shared parenting. "The idea that children must belong wholly or even essentially to one (and only one set of individuals/parents) is just the sort of fiction that many adoption services, public or 'commercial' promote—those, in particular that advocate planary adoption in which children are 'de-socialized', given a 'clean slate' by administratively erasing all pre-adoption history" (Fonseca 2003a).

Here interest in transnational adoption coincides with policies of the "clean-break" model where all ties to biological family are severed. Families who prefer this model are therefore assumed to be choosing transnational adoption rather than succumb to greater legal restraints of domestic adoption. "The irony is that it is exactly those alternatives that, for a variety of reasons are most common in Europe and North American—institutional and foster care—that are effectively denigrated in the arena of intercountry adoption" (Fonseca 2003a).

A mechanism for middle-class family-building in the United States, private/intercountry adoption fits neatly within the new global reality with its attention to individual and family welfare, favoring those with adequate funds or the ability to secure $10,000–$40,000 in adoption loans. Though not explicit or even intended, private/intercountry adoption is another vehicle of privilege masked by benevolent rhetoric. Adoption is not only an ancient practice but also has the benefit of being regarded as an altruistic one, at least since the twentieth century. Most adoption institutions—for example, orphanages in sending countries and private agencies in receiving countries—maintain a not-for-profit status. Of course this ignores informal practices such as bribes or fees for expedited adoption that occur in intercountry adoption. Adoption activist Ellen Fitzrider rightly asks why it costs $20,000 or more to adopt a child in a country where the annual per capita income is less than $400 a year. Even though private/intercountry adoption serves a relatively small fraction of the world's needy children, the formal and informal practices of private/intercountry adoption contribute millions to the global economy as asymmetric economic and power relations situate children within the international order of countries sending and receiving them (Lieberthal 2001).[2] Regardless of the method of migration or the good intentions of some participants, children are often brought to the United States (and other receiving countries) through the use of unscrupulous or unethical means—stolen, sold, smuggled—and even adopted.

The only developed country to prefer private adoption over adoption through public agencies, the United States has been slow to adopt the Hague

Convention Treaty (Masson 2001).[3] Written in 1993 and signed by over forty countries, the treaty represents an international effort to reduce the abuses of children and provide a framework within which participating nations can work. Although the United States signed the Convention in 1994, and President Clinton signed the Intercountry Adoption Act to implement the Convention in 2000, the treaty has yet to be ratified. Anticipated ratification is in 2007 or 2008, when the State Department will become the Central Authority on intercountry adoptions and issue standards, accredit agencies, and maintain records for Congress. As the largest receiving country of children through private/intercountry adoption, the United States' procrastination in implementing the treaty may promote similar behavior among other countries and calls into question our commitment to children. Our country has also engaged in pressuring sending countries that place moratoriums on intercountry adoption (Romania, Guatemala, Liberia). The context of private adoption is where abuses are most likely to occur, prompting UNICEF (n.d.; United Nations Children's Fund) to assess it as "high risk": "Over the past 30 years, the number of families from wealthy countries wanting to adopt children from other countries has grown substantially. At the same time, lack of regulation and oversight, particularly in the countries of origin, coupled with the potential for financial gain, has spurred the growth of an industry around adoption, where profit, rather than the best interests of children, takes centre stage. Abuses include the sale and abduction of children, coercion of parents, and bribery, as well as trafficking to individuals whose intentions are to exploit rather than care for children."

Unfortunately, the Hague Treaty continues to allow private/intercountry adoption facilitated by both not-for-profit and for-profit agencies. And although countries have been modifying their practices, the continuing dominant philosophy (and one no doubt influenced by receiving countries) is that market mechanisms work effectively to assure that only reputable agencies and good practices prevail (Masson 2001).

How does race factor into this picture? Past and present racism (and classism) are two of the variables affecting the status of children within and between nations. Neoliberal ideology and social policy construct identities of foreign children as abandoned, unwanted, and freely placed. Transnational, or intercountry, adoption then becomes a global humanitarian effort. In this context race is made irrelevant in what is really a racialized global market system. Psychologist Richard Lee (2003) reveals the root of transnational adoption as slavery, where apprenticeship, assimilation, and utilitarian models became modes of transnational (and domestic) adoption. History of the adoption arena is not only illustrative of U.S. racial conflicts; patterns of transnational adoption can also be seen as aligning with what Howard Winant (2004) calls the "re-racialization" of the world. Ongoing resistance of nation states to intercountry adoption (e.g., Brazil, Guatemala) in the face of collapsing or transitioning market economies signals continuing tensions between globalization processes, nationalism, and race. From receiving countries' standpoint, resistance to transnational adoption represents nothing less than a perverse lack of caring for children. From the perspective of several sending countries, however, nationalistic adoption movements and resistance to adoption by foreigners is a point of national honor and represents protection of citizens from human rights abuses. Struggles involving transnational adoption between the United States and other nations contain all the elements reflective of other geopolitical struggles within and between states: race, class, nativity, and identity. Some critics argue that, ultimately, outcomes of intercountry adoption laws reflect the interests of "First World" adoptive parents, and these interests do not generally stimulate increased legal restrictions and protective mechanisms for families (and children) from sending countries (Fonseca 2003a; Trenka, et al. 2006).

Racialized structures and subjective constructions of children articulate with intercountry adoption as racial/ethnic status generates *racialized* symbolic capital affecting the life chances of those possessing it (e.g., light skin)— in this case, desirability for adoption. Discourses involving children from other countries promote different responses from adoptive parents to similar circumstances of children, such as poverty, physical or emotional health problems, or developmental delay. Children are framed either as remediable (intercountry adoptees) or as "lost cause" or beyond salvation (children from the U.S. underclass) (Ortiz and Briggs 2003). Both discourses reify a shifting but racialized structure in the United States.

We need to reconsider the argument that various forms of adoption (transracial, minority, intercountry) promote transnational identities and result in blurring racial/ethnic boundaries. Instead, these practices can be seen as colonial projects, absorbing and transforming the "other" into non-other. While it is true that some adoptees can change their class position and become

honorary members of the dominant culture, particularly white racial and eth-
nically European children, research findings are mixed and suggest that racialization processes are perceived differently as adoptees age (R. Lee 2003;
Freundlich and Lieberthal 2000). Assumptions and promises to the contrary,
private/intercountry adoption not only fails to address the needs of the majority of children in sending nations but also contributes to the reconfiguring
of race in the United States (and increasingly the world). To borrow from Toni
Morrison's analogy of Clarence Thomas and the character Friday in *Robinson
Crusoe*, many adoptees feel the pressure of owing allegiance to the "master":
"Voluntary entrance into another culture, voluntary sharing of more than one
culture, has certain satisfaction to mitigate the problems that might ensue. But
being rescued into an adversarial culture can carry a huge debt. This debt one
feels one owes to the rescuer can be paid, simply, honorably, in lifetime service. . . . Under such circumstances it is not just easy to speak the master's language, it is necessary" (Morrison 1992).

By recognizing the colonial aspects of private/intercountry adoption we
can also begin to challenge practices that reproduce racial, gendered, and economic hierarchies. Unless substantial efforts are made to alter who partici-
pates in discussions of children's rights, the prospects for conceptualizing
"global" human rights apart from the exercising of individual rights are not
very good. In chapter 3, the racial history of American adoption sheds light on
how historic and contemporary adoption policies intersect with race and affect persons of color.

NOTES

1. In its report *Trafficking for Sexual Exploitation* (International Organization for
Migration n.d.), the United Nations estimated that 1.2 million children are trafficked
each year.

2. In testimony before the House Committee on International Relations, Cindy
Friedmutter, executive director of the Evan B. Donaldson Adoption Institute,
estimated that U.S. adoptive parents spent close to $200 million in 2001 for
international adoption services. Peter Selman (2001) suggests that the number of
intercountry adoptions is higher than many estimates and that it is now at its highest
level worldwide, with these numbers projected to increase in the near future. This
projection contradicts a prior claim by Simon and Altstein (1991) who argued that

the phenomenon of nonwhite children from poor nations being "transferred" to wealthy white nations was on the decline and would continue to decline.

3. In 2000, President Bill Clinton signed the Intercountry Adoption Act, which would eventually ratify the Hague Convention Treaty by the United States. As of June 2006, the treaty had yet to be ratified.

3

Racial Projects and the Changing Discourse of Adoption

In the past three decades, changes in U.S. society have found their way into the adoption arena, resulting in new laws, policies, and participants in the adoption process and altering the discourse of adoption. "Minimum standards" that define who gets adopted and who adopts have been broadened to include children from other countries, single and older adoptive parents, children with special needs, gay adoptive parents, children adopted by parents of another race, and even the adoption of embryos. This chapter examines the cultural and historic logic of adoption and discursive constructions within the adoption arena, specifically constructions of race. Race is observed as a sociopolitical construct situated in a particular historical moment and intersecting with different social movements that influenced adoption.

Adoption discourse is part of the larger processes of racial formation occurring in the United States that led to symbolic violence against children of color, namely African Americans.[1] Child welfare projects generally, and early adoption in particular, were embedded within larger racial projects designed to protect the security of a "white" country and its families.[2] Critical events such as World War II and the subsequent formation of African American placement agencies contributed to widening the scope of adoption, but not until the civil rights and women's liberation movements intersected to generate major social transformations in society did race emerge at the forefront of public consciousness and in the adoption arena. Social transformations were limited, however, and though the discourse of modern adoption has shifted, the legacy of adoption regarding race remains. Adoption language and policies continue to highlight the questionable role of race in adoption and instantiate relations of power in the larger society. A look at current attempts to reconstruct adoption draws on adoption literature and information in the public domain to show how despite the current discourse of equity in contemporary adoption, children of color, particularly African American children, continue to be marginalized in the adoption market as bargain-basement deals.

CULTURAL TEXTS

In *Dancing with Bigotry*, Donaldo Macedo and Lillia Bartolome (2001) point out that the popular press and mass media educate more people about issues of race and ethnicity than all other sources of education combined. Believing this to be the case with adoption, I gathered information from a variety of sources. Added to the scholarly work on adoption were references on adoption language and policy such as the *Encyclopedia of Adoption* (2000) and the on-line *Adoption Glossary and Terminology* (2005), along with a sample of current adoption books written by adoption experts. Three of the books are presented here: *Adoption Nation* (2000), by Adam Pertman (director of the Evan B. Donaldson Institute); *Making Sense of Adoption* (1989), by Lois Melina; and *Adoption Is a Family Affair* (2004), by Patricia Irwin Johnston.[3]

I also looked at the Internet, which has become a major source of adoption information and where literally hundreds of websites are available for all participants in the adoption process. Adoption organizations and foundations (Dave Thomas Foundation, Evan B. Donaldson Institute on Adoption, National Adoption Information Clearinghouse, North American Council on Adoptable Children) make information readily available through websites providing links to numerous other sites in the adoption network. An online public resource, *The Adoption History Project* (Herman n.d.), includes primary documents. Also included are eight websites on adoption language sponsored by different adoption groups, and a sample of twenty-four private infant adoption agency websites (eight "color-blind," eight "potentially color-blind," and eight with explicit racial/ethnic programs; see chapter 4 for a detailed explanation of these categories). Each text was examined for its current adoption policy and language content, with specific attention given to race.

Interpreted both as a device for categorization and as discursive formation, the language of adoption empowers some groups and disempowers others.

ADOPTION, CHILD WELFARE, AND EUGENICS (1900–1960)

Early twentieth-century adoption involved a preoccupation with the inherited deficiencies of "illegitimate" children shared by persons placing and adopting them. At that time, children generally and adoptive children in particular were caught in the vortex of social forces shifting how they were treated legally and socially. Two social movements aligned and became instrumental in shaping early adoption practices: the child welfare reform movement and the eugenics movement. These two movements reflected the prevailing ideology of race and its enduring impact on adoption policies and practices for persons of color (see table 3.1).

The child welfare reform movement represented both an ideological and a religious response to the many social transformations occurring at the turn of the century: massive immigration, industrialization, rapid urbanization, and wide-scale poverty (Cremin 1988; Lindemeyer 1997). It was the goal of reformers to create the Kingdom of God here on earth, and they were going to begin by saving children. Securing legal protection for children required first a revision of their social location from economically useful and productive workers to sacred and priceless gifts (Zelizer 1985). Ultimately, it became more difficult to engage young children in paid labor and inappropriate to leave them without families and homes. Within the first three decades, this movement had successfully redefined children and family. Indeed, without children there was no "family"— merely childless couples (May 1995). Evolving from these comprehensive attempts at child protection were some of the first standards for adoption mandated by court decisions, state laws, newly formed adoption agencies, and private and government organizations (e.g., Child Welfare League of America) (Smith and Merkel-Holguin 1995).

The changing definition of children was simultaneous with a period of rampant xenophobia, grounded in the myth of white Protestant superiority and nativeness. Having excluded black children entirely from services or segregated them into inferior programs (Billingsley and Giovannoni 1972), the child welfare reform movement both aligned with and confronted another movement whose goal was to secure the white middle class by promoting sanctity of blood ties (i.e., "natural parents"): the eugenics movement. The

Table 3.1. Adoption, Child Welfare, and Eugenics Movements Timeline

	Adoption	Child Welfare	Eugenics
1907			First eugenic sterilization law passed in Indiana
1909	First national conference Care of Dependent Children	First national conference Care of Dependent Children	
1911			Eugenics Record Office established
1912		U.S. Children's Bureau created	First mass use of standardized IQ test in United States
1914			First national conference on Race Betterment (Battle Creek, MI); Foundation for Race Betterment established
1915		Bureau for Exchange of Information Among Child-Helping Organizations created	
1916	Issue of feeblemindedness of adoptive children emerged and use of IQ test as part of adoption process emerged		
1917	First law mandating home studies for adoptions and confidentiality of adoption records (Minnesota)		U.S. Army administers IQ tests to 1.7 million recruits
1918			The Galton Society established (a group of academics and funders endorsing racist policies in American society)
1920	Matching became adoption policy (1920–1970)	Child Welfare League of America established	
1919–1929	Russell Sage Foundation publishes first child-placing manual; American Association of Social Workers founded; first empirical studies of adoption; founding of adoption agencies Spence Alumni Society, the Cradle, and Alice Chapin Nursery	U.S. Children's Bureau sets minimum standards for child placing	Harry Laughlin appointed expert eugenics agent for the House Committee on Immigration and Naturalization

Year		
1924	First major outcome study of adoption published	Immigration Restriction Act and Virginia Act to Preserve Racial Integrity passed
1925		American Eugenics Society founded
1929		Human Betterment Foundation established (largely focused on sterilization)
1934	Iowa administers mental tests to adoptive children to assess feeblemindedness	
1935	Social Security Act establishes Aid to Dependent Children and child welfare services	South Carolina passes eugenic sterilization law (thirty-first state to do so); Nazi Nuremberg laws passed (modeled in part on antimiscegenation laws)
1938	Fair Labor Standards Act outlaws child labor	
1939		Eugenics Record Office closes (Carnegie Foundation pulls funding)
1948	First recorded transracial adoption of African American child by white parents (Minnesota)	
1958	Child Welfare League publishes Standards of Adoption Service (revised in 1968, '73, '78, '88, 2000)	
1953–1958	First national effort to locate adoptive homes for African American children	
1957	U.S. adoption agencies sponsor legislation to prohibit/control "proxy"/international adoptions	
1959	General Assembly of the United Nations adopts Declaration of the Rights of the Child	
1967		Supreme Court strikes down the Racial Integrity Act of 1924 (VA) along with fifteen states' antimiscegenation laws
1972		Last of eugenic state sterilization laws removed

eugenics movement's emphasis on heredity and anxieties about "race suicide" (the fear that whites would be outnumbered by nonwhites), were reflected in attempts to reform child welfare laws and practices, including those of a nascent adoption industry (Kline 2001; Sallee 2004).[4] Part of a racist ideology that permeated all areas of civic and social life, racial policies such as Jim Crow statutes and the Immigration Restriction Act gained new momentum at the same time that the adoption industry was being established. Racist ideology undergirding such policies included assumptions that (1) races existed in a hierarchy with whites physically and mentally superior to others; (2) race caused culture and culture was genetically transmitted; (3) race determined personality and temperament; and therefore, (4) race mixing reduced the purity and biological quality of the "superior" race (Davis 1991).

Still, a significant segment of eugenics proponents were also strongly in favor of carefully planned adoptions through which children deemed worthy could be placed into white middle-class homes that would provide proper Americanizing influences and opportunities. Whether by design or default, the goals of child welfare reformers and proponents of eugenics often coalesced to generate a variety of practices in adoption that included personality and intelligence testing and matching. To child welfare reformers, eugenics proponents, and, ultimately, adoption professionals, the scientific model ensured optimal family-making, minimizing risks by ensuring that children met clearly defined specifications. With unapologetic ardor, psychometric and genetic testing and medicine were used to engage in utopian social engineering of families (Gill 2000). Each added a patina of legitimacy to the professionalization of adoption and became embedded in the minimum standards of adoption agencies for decades. In this way, adoption presented one mode of controlling family formation.

MATCHING

The positive connotation behind matching was to model the "real" or "normal" family so well that the family created through adoption would be indistinguishable from other families.[5] A number of criteria were used in identifying and joining adoptive parents with children, such as physical features, religion, and temperament; however, one of the most important considerations in matching was race. According to several sources, race served as the most "firmly institutionalized form of matching" (Ladner 1977; Melosh 2002; Stack

1974; Modell and Dambaucher 1997; Freundlich 1998; Gordon 1999), and if no one questioned the superiority of biological or natural families to adoptive ones, surely no one questioned the superiority of the white family to families of color. In historical context discursive practices of adoption reflected stereotypes (what Fregoso [2003] calls a central strategy of colonial discourse) that dominated the United States. Children of color were viewed as marginal and their "natural" inferiority presumed. Adoptive status only served to magnify what were already firmly entrenched assumptions about these children by members of the dominant society. Adopting children of color, particularly African American children, represented the outer limits of acceptance as racist representational strategies involving stereotypes of sexual depravity, poor temperament, and feeblemindedness were presumed to be innate to these children. A range of other derogatory representations was widely available, especially for mixed-race children. These children were regarded as "impulsive, unstable, and prone to insanity" (Raymond Paredes, as cited in Fregoso 2003). Interracial children implicitly challenged racial boundaries and systems of representation. Presenting an alternative to the existing racial hierarchy, cross-racial and interracial adoption exposed the racial homogeneity of the nation's identity and threatened the sanctity of its white families. Interracial or "cross-racial" adoption, therefore, was regarded as a subversive act challenging social control of the system.

Directly and indirectly, the child welfare and eugenics movements played a part in shaping adoption—efforts to remove children from the labor market, mandate compulsory education, and sustain the family interacted with an emphasis on innate abilities, personality, and presumed racial/ethnic characteristics. Policies supported by advocates of both movements affected decisions on which children merited placement and which couples merited children. Both movements relied heavily upon socially constructed discourses of groups whose cultural "otherness" served to reify whiteness as superior and as synonymous with national identity. Indeed, the discourse of adoption throughout much of the twentieth century was one of white "native" Anglo-Saxon supremacy. Social constructions of poor children, immigrants, and racial/ethnic groups of color as lower on the social and intellectual ladder profoundly served to legitimatize racist and class-based practices that occurred not only in adoption but also in other areas of society at that time. World War II brought an end to professional endorsement of eugenics and early adoption practices gave way to more enlightened views regarding child welfare. Still, the ideology that dominated early twentieth century thinking regarding children of color prevailed through subsequent decades as matching continued to guide infant placements, particularly when it came to race and religion (Herman 2002). Though not explicitly racial in its goals, adoption reflected the views of society, and contributed to shaping the racial experience of children.

ADOPTION, CIVIL RIGHTS, AND WOMEN'S LIBERATION (1960–2000)

Just as early adoption practices can be linked to the child welfare and eugenics movements, changes in these practices can be seen as influenced by two modern movements: the civil rights and women's liberation movements. Though interracial adoption began in the 1950s, it was not until the civil rights movement and the movements that followed that ideas regarding race and ethnicity were effectively challenged (see table 3.2).

The successes of the civil rights movement and other racial/ethnic movements of the 1960s (e.g., the Chicano and Native American movements) disrupted the notion of a national identity based on whiteness as racism became part of the public discourse. One of the many legacies of the civil rights and women's liberation movements is that professionals and policy makers began to rethink their practices regarding children of color. To comprehend the relationship between the ideological construct of racism, the ways in which it shaped adoption practices for ethnic children, and how this construct was ultimately challenged, the cultural conditions that gave rise to this challenge must be reconstructed.

Segregation, Miscegenation, and Integration

Despite the Reconstruction period following the Civil War, by the late nineteenth century, the U.S. Supreme Court had nullified the gains made by blacks with its 1883 ruling reversing the 1875 Civil Rights Act, which had guaranteed equal access to all public facilities, regardless of race. This decision provided the impetus for Southern legislatures to pass a variety of segregation statutes that ultimately became known as the Jim Crow system of segregation. Jim Crow statutes ranged from separate seating in public places to separate schools and other public facilities to laws that prohibited interracial marriage. What began as legally enforced sanctions against miscegenation in the South evolved into a system adhered to throughout the country by both whites and blacks. In the South, Jim Crow sanctions were manifested as de jure segregation while in the North, de facto segregation in public facilities, housing, and jobs made opportunities for race mixing few and infrequent (Davis 1991).

Racist ideology justifying the Jim Crow system of segregation held sway within adoption for this same historical period when African American children were regarded as unwanted by white adoptive couples and unattainable by black adoptive couples. Not only had a system of informal adoption been embraced by the African American community, but black adoptive couples typically experienced prejudice and discrimination at the hands of child welfare and adoption agencies. These experiences discouraged pursuits of formal adoption (Patton 2000; Billingsley and Giovannoni 1972; Berebitsky 2000).[6]

Ironically, as the 1960s and 1970s saw a shift in public consciousness and increased white acceptance of transracial adoption (of black and biracial infants), a shift also occurred in African American consciousness—but in the opposite direction. A significant segment of blacks modified their position on assimilation as a means of gaining equality in America and opposed miscegenation. Transracial adoption was regarded as destructive to racial solidarity (Melosh 2002).

Nevertheless, the mere fact of domestic transracial adoptions was a watershed in race relations as a small but significant number of whites resisted hegemonic representations of race and family. Just as the civil rights movement challenged racial assumptions, the women's movement simultaneously called into question a variety of assumptions about the values and organization of society.

Women's Liberation

As feminists fought the sociopolitical and economic oppression of women, institutions that secured or reproduced that oppression were challenged, among them, marriage, work, and the family. Targeting issues of reproductive rights, pay equity, and gender discrimination, women sought to broaden their roles and opportunities outside the home. Changing norms allowed women to successfully redefine what it meant to be a woman as the stigma attached to being unmarried, a single mother, or a working woman and mother diminished. Social and political forces ultimately converged to change family forms that continue to evolve today (Berkeley 1999; Freeman 1982). Whereas

Table 3.2. Adoption and the Civil Rights and Women's Liberation Movements Timeline

	Adoption	Civil Rights	Women's Liberation
1960	Published study claims adopted children one hundred times more likely to show up in clinical populations	President Eisenhower signs the Civil Rights Act	Food and Drug Adminstration approves birth control pills
1963		More than 250,000 demonstrators march on Washington, D.C.; Martin Luther King, Jr. delivers "I Have a Dream" speech	Betty Friedan's *Feminine Mystique* published
1964		24th Amendment outlaws poll Tax; Civil Rights Act passes	Civil Rights Act bars discrimination based on sex; establishes EEOC (Equal Employment Opportunity, Commission), which receives fifty thousand complaints of gender discrimination in first 5 years
1965	First organized program of single-parent adoptions to locate homes for hard-to-place children	Malcolm X assassinated; Riots in Watts	
1966	National Adoption Resource Exchange established	Edward W. Brooke (MA) first black senator since Reconstruction	National Organization of Women established
1968		Martin Luther King Jr. assassinated; LBJ signs Housing Act	First national women's liberation conference; National Abortion Rights Action League established; Shirley Chisolm elected to U.S. Congress
1970	Adoptions reach peak at 175,000 (80 percent arranged by agencies)	Senate extends Voting Rights Act banning literacy tests	Equal Rights Amendment reintroduced into Congress
1971	Adoptees' Liberty Movement Association's goal to abolish sealed records		
1972	National Association of Black Social Workers oppose transracial adoption		
1973			*Roe v. Wade* legalizes abortion; the first battered women's shelters open; Billie Jean King beats Bobby Riggs in tennis

Year			
1974			Women's Studies courses offered in colleges; First time in history that more women than men enter college
1978	Indian Child Welfare Act		
1980	Adoption Assistance and Child Welfare Act (subsidizing special needs adoptions)	Supreme Court rules that intentional discrimination must be proven to declare an election unconstitutional	
1981			Sandra Day O'Connor first woman appointed to the Supreme Court
1983–1989		Martin Luther King Jr's birthday declared national holiday; Vanessa Williams first black Miss America; Rev. Jesse Jackson places second in Democratic presidential race; Colin Powell first black Chief of Staff for U.S. Armed Forces; Congress passes Civil Rights Bill	Geraldine Ferraro first woman vice-presidential candidate
1990–1995	Hague Convention (protection of children in intercountry adoption); Multiethnic Placement Act followed by Interethnic Placement Act prohibits denying transracial adoptions (first federal law to concern itself with race in adoption)	Anita Hill testifies that Clarence Thomas sexually harassed her; Los Angeles police accused of beating Rodney King found not guilty;	Take Our Daughters to Work Day; Women are paid 71¢ for every dollar paid to men; black women earn 65¢; Latina women 54¢.
1996	Bastard Nation founded (concerned with obtaining access to sealed records)	Ebonics use in schools sparks national debate	
1997	Adoption and Safe Families Act (shift from family reunification toward adoption)		
1998	Ballot Measure 58 (OR) allows adult adoptees access to original birth certificates		
2000	Child Citizenship Act of 2000 (allows foreign-born adoptees to become automatic citizens upon entering United States); U.S. Census 2000 includes adopted son/daughter category for first time in U.S. history	Colin Powell becomes first black U.S. secretary of state	

adoption professionals had traditionally defined family as "white middle-class heterosexual married couples with children," modification of normative structures in society forced a broadening of the concept in adoption. In the latter part of the twentieth century more and more persons/couples delayed childbirth and experienced infertility, and more single women and same-sex couples sought to build families through adoption. These realities were matched by cultural and demographic changes that exacerbated a decline in white infants placed for adoption: the legalization of abortion, increased availability and use of contraceptives, and the increased acceptance of single and/or teen parenting (Abma et al. 1997; Chandra et al. 1999; Bacharach, London, and Maza 1991; Solinger 1992, 2001). Consequently, the adoption industry reinvented itself both as an altruistic effort toward social betterment and with the goal of remaining a viable institution in a changing society. What followed was a new discourse of adoption that opened the field to new participants and reflected greater sensitivity. Shifting adoption discourse also reflected an emergent racial reality that opened the door for what was now called *transracial* adoption. Transracial adoption had existed prior to this time; however, most adoptions involved children from other countries such as Korea and although transracial adoption is not new (African Americans have engaged in transracial adoption for decades, accepting biracial children when the vast majority of whites refused to consider them), the term took on new meaning once white couples sought children of other racial/ethnic groups (Patton 2000; Melosh 2002). The new discourse now portrayed adoption of these children as an enhancement of the lives of adopters and adoptees, a significant change from historical descriptions of physicians and scientists intervening to assure social workers and adoptive couples of the identity of racially ambiguous infants.

Opposed by black activists and the National Association of Black Social Workers, domestic transracial adoptions substantially diminished in the 1970s and 1980s, though it was not long before racial matching policies were challenged by white adoptive couples and foster parents. Early adoption matching centered on optimizing adoptive family characteristics with the adoptee. Matching also maintained separation of racial/ethnic groups. Prior to the 1950s few people worried about the plight of African American orphans. In the context of changing demographics, however, the argument was one of discrimination, and African Americans who opposed transracial adoption were accused of wanting race-conscious policy that failed to benefit children. Though unacknowledged, the main difference was who was being discriminated against (i.e., whites). Challenges to matching resulted in the Multi-Ethnic and Inter-Ethnic Placement Acts (MEPA-IEP) of 1994 and 1996, which prohibited public or state-supported private agencies from denying or delaying adoption placement based on race and thus secured the rights of white adoptive couples (the dominant group of adoptive couples) by legally abolishing matching. These laws reversed the traditional stance taken by adoption professionals, courts, and the general population, which had maintained social, political, and legal sanctions for race mixing. A discourse of reverse discrimination and the welfare of black children insisted on the moral irrelevance of race, yet applied primarily to adoptive parents (Bradley and Hawkins-Leon 2002). In other words, a racial preference stated by black birth parents could not be considered in placement of children.

THE "NEW" ADOPTION DISCOURSE: REARTICULATING RACE? (1980–2004)

Remarkably adoption language did not change in the 1960s or even in the 1970s, when several counterdiscourses were beginning to reshape normative structures and social policies. Respectful Adoption Language (RAL) (also known as Constructive Adoption Language and Positive Adoption Language) did not emerge until the 1980s. Some attribute origins of the new language to a single enlightened social worker, while others claim adoptive parents, fatigued with the social response and secondary status of their families, developed a new language (Johnston 2004; Fancott 1997). What is apparent in the past twenty-five years is a shift in the discursive practices of adoption to broaden acceptance of adoptive families. Old terminology (e.g., blue-ribbon babies, natural parents, illegitimate, unadoptable, feebleminded) has given way to a set of kinder, more inclusive terms. Most private adoption agencies, magazines, articles, and books illustrate these changes. Several sources provide simple lists of "old" or "negative" language juxtaposed against "new" or "positive" language, which seeks to modify assumptions, images, and attitudes.

Attempts to change adoption discourse have also met with resistance. For example, Exiled Mothers Concerned United Birthparents (mothers who placed or were coerced into relinquishing their children) have expressed opposition to the new adoption language in a challenge to the industry: "The adoption industry has deliberately constructed and marketed a lexicon that is meant to marginalize natural mothers and dehumanize them, giving legitimacy to a form of inhumane exploitation that would otherwise be seen as cruel and unnatural. . . . The language thing is much more than a gimmick or novelty. It is a tool of oppression. Groups that control the lexicon can control a society's thinking subversively."

This idea resonates with Barbara Katz Rothman's struggle with the ways in which women become mothers in our postmodern society as she concludes that in spite of our most valiant efforts, the language of consumerism dominates virtually everything in the United States. No matter how we may consciously try to separate and insulate our human relationships from the cold invisible hand of the marketplace, "adoption becomes an exercise in thoughtful comparative shopping" (Rothman, 2005, 52). Still, it is difficult to know how well modern adoption language is integrated into American vernacular.

To understand how the language of race in adoption has evolved, I looked at resources of adoption terminology and a number of books written by the leading adoption experts (see note 3). Glossaries and dictionaries of adoption terminology have relatively limited numbers of entries addressing race (see table 3.3). Unlike attempts to soften harsher images evoked by descriptors like *handicapped* and *feebleminded* (replaced with *special needs*) or *foreign* (changed to *international* and *intercountry*), no similar approach for race was found in these resources.

Instead, old terms like *interracial* and *mixed-race* are replaced with *biracial*, and *cross-racial* adoption is now referred to as *transracial* adoption, yet definitions of these terms remain the same. In *The Encyclopedia of Adoption* (Adamec and Pierce 2000) transracial "properly refers to any adoption across racial or ethnic lines, including what are probably the most frequent transracial adoptions in the United States—adoptions of Asian children by white parents." Later in the entry we learn that transracial "generally" refers to the adoption of black or biracial children by white adoptive families. Whatever its technical definition, "black children and white parents have always defined the debate about transracial adoption, achieving a symbolic importance that overshadowed their tiny numbers" (Herman n.d.).

Language formerly used by social workers to describe adoptive children and prospective parents reveals the negotiation of power and authority. It also illustrates the adoption industry's traditional role in racial identification and

Table 3.3.   Race in Adoption Glossaries

Encyclopedia of Adoption, 2nd ed. (Adamec and Pierce 2000).
400 cross-referenced entries (14 race-related entries)
    Biracial; black adoptive parent recruitment programs; black families; culture camps;
    interracial; Korean adopted children; Latin American children; multiethnic; matching;
    multiethnic placement act; race; rainbow families; skin color; transracial adoption
    * Cocaine and crack babies; hard-to-place children; special needs; unadoptable; waiting
    children

"Adoption Glossary" (1995–2005). http://glossary.adoption.com
267 entries (6 race-related entries)
    Primary Focus/Theme: biracial adoptions; Inter-Ethnic Placement; multiethnic
    adoptions; Multi-Ethnic Placement Act of 1994; multiracial adoptions; trans-
    racial adoptions
    * Special needs

National Adoption Information Clearinghouse glossary http://naic.acf.hhs.gov/admin/
glossary.cfm
157 entries (2 race-related entries)
    Multi-Ethnic Placement Act; Inter-Ethnic Placement Act
    * Special needs

The Adoption History Project (Herman n.d.). http://darkwing.uoregon.edu/~adoption/
topics/index.html
35 entries (5 race-related entries)
    African American adoptions; *The Family Nobody Wanted*, 1954; Indian Child Welfare
    Act; Indian Adoption Project; transracial adoptions
    * Fostering and foster care; special-needs adoptions

* Categories associated with race.

placement of children. In her study of transracial adoptees, Sandra Patton referred to a written description of an adoptee's two possible fathers:

"Each man was unproblematically considered black or white, and once this
had been established, the categories were maintained through the adjectives
chosen to describe the two men, who looked alike. The German—read
white—man was 'dark with frizzy hair,' and the black man was 'light-skinned.'
In a society structured by a different racial order, these two men might have
been considered members of the same race" (Patton 2000, 37).

New adoption discourse also includes words that serve as code for *race.*
Nonracially specific descriptors such as "cocaine and crack babies" continue to
conjure racial images created by society and sustained by the media. At the
close of a lengthy entry on drug abuse (cross-listed with "cocaine and crack
babies"), the *Encyclopedia of Adoption* addresses the lack of a racial division
between pregnant women using drugs but concludes that African American

women are "ten times more likely to be charged with drug abuse" (Adamec and Pierce 2000). Race is configured and reconfigured in the discourse of adoption as texts are meant to shift yet in subtle ways reify the racialization of children, thus signaling adoption as both site of resistance and accommodation.

Children used to be labeled "unadoptable" (now "hard to place" or "special needs") because of their age, physical or mental limitations, or race. Now African American (and in one region of the country, Latino) children get sorted into special needs programs through descriptions like the following from the Florida Baptist Children's Home: "Typically they are over age 8, have emotional or physical disabilities, are a minority, or are part of a sibling group that should not be separated." Creative Adoptions also provides examples of children in the agency's Special Needs category (in order): two boys whose mothers used drugs and alcohol, a blind baby, premature infants with severe medical complications, four African American infants, twelve biracial infants, a severely retarded baby, and two infants with Downs Syndrome. Even when agencies identify African American and biracial children as "healthy minority newborns placed directly with us by their birthparents for the purposes of adoption" or "healthy newborn infants directly from the hospital," these infants are either placed in separate minority programs or adopted through special needs programs. Despite the change in wording; the health, age, physical status; or any other complicating factors, a child only has to be black to be "hard to place" or "special needs." Heritage Adoption Services, a private agency website, assures adoptive parents in its "Important Diversity Program Facts" page that "the majority of newborn babies through the Diversity Program are African American. Most are healthy babies, non–drug addicted." Such caveats are both a product of and response to racial stereotypes as resources of adoption terminology illustrate how even attempts to resist myths of racial identity fail to avoid the political implications of race.

Since sources of adoption terminology are only one type of resource and limited in their content, examination of popular books written by adoption experts provide an additional gauge of how race is constructed and reconstructed in adoption (see table 3.4). Despite efforts to challenge existing hierarchies and power structures texts often invoke racial identity (explanation of what makes a child from one sociocultural group different from a central point of reference). Issues of multiculturalism and transracial adoption are

Table 3.4.   Race in Popular Adoption Books

Adoption Nation (Pertman 2000). 349 pp.
Adoption through ethnic and cultural diversity; transracial adoptions; special needs; black adoptive parents; high price of Caucasian babies; diversity of families; shortage of Native American parents; Institute for Black Parenting; color, ethnicity, and age; affects on Korean adoptees; Multiethnic Placement Act.

Making Sense of Adoption (Melina 1984). 277 pp.
1.5 pages on child's heritage; 2 pages on minority family; 12.5 pages on racial awareness, prejudice and nationality, and culture camps; 5.5 pages on racial identity, transracial adoption, interracial relationships, and discussing racial issues (21.5 pages total)

Adoption as a Family Affair (Johnston 2001). 151 pp.
2-page section entitled "What about Race?" (brief discussion of racism with recommended books and website); over 2 pages on racism; 14 quotations of racist comments associated with the stigma of adoption (4 pages total)

highlighted in order to transcend borders of race; however, they also reinforce these borders as those who possess power are typically constructed as "subject" (adopter) while those without resources (adoptee) are constructed as "object" or other—that which is acted upon.

Patricia Irwin Johnston's *Adoption Is a Family Affair* (2001) offers evidence of the limited impact of new adoption language and the continued color consciousness of Americans. Johnston's book focuses on defining and supporting the role of nuclear and extended family in the adoption process. From personal experience and in discussion with others, Johnston acknowledges how perceptions about adoption and race interact to generate awkward and inappropriate situations for adoptive families. Using fourteen quotations of insensitive racial/ethnic comments and questions directed at adoptive parents, Johnston presents transracial adoption as a discursive struggle between adopters and strangers, friends, and family.

Lois Melina (1989) gives considerably more attention to these issues, presenting adoption language as an ongoing discursive practice that configures and reconfigures race across time and place. In *Making Sense of Adoption*, Melina delves into the dilemmas of transracial and multiethnic families and offers approaches to parenting.

The enormously popular *Adoption Nation* (Pertman 2000), includes candid and extensive discussion of race (if a somewhat naive projection of the decline of racial categories and racism) and recognizes transracial adoption as transgressing the social and political borders of race. In fact, it is difficult to find a modern adoption book that completely ignores race. However, few authors (with the exception of Pertman) deal with the conundrum of race and adoption in any substantive way, other than to advise adoptive parents on the "dilemmas" involved in raising racial/ethnic children. Clearly, complex issues like race, culture, and acceptance can never be adequately addressed in books providing practical information on a multitude of topics; however, when adoption expert and parent of a Peruvian child Mary Best-Hopkins (*Toddler Adoption*, 1997) devotes a mere four pages of text to the interaction of race/ethnicity and age, these issues are divorced from issues of selection (of toddlers versus infants), entitlement, attachment, and physical, cognitive and emotional development of children. However inadvertently, race is made a nonissue. Recognition of the need to educate parents about the responsibilities and challenges they are taking on in transracial adoption represents more than the valuing of diversity. It is an admission that ours is not a color-blind society, which makes the superficial treatment of racial matters in popular adoption literature even more troublesome. Equally important, language is not used consistently across adoption sources as some experts (and websites) continue to use terminology that others regard as passé or insensitive (e.g., mixed-race, handicapped; see table 3.5). Adoption texts illustrate how constructions of race in adoption resonate with and challenge existing racialized power structures.

THE LANGUAGE OF RACE ON PRIVATE AGENCY WEBSITES

Much of adoption language has been changed to appear more inclusive of groups traditionally restricted from adoption, such as single persons, older couples, and "alternative" families (i.e., gay and lesbian). Beyond promoting transracial adoption, however, an example of the limited alteration of racial discourse in adoption is evident on the Internet. Web pages of private adoption agencies signal a prevailing ambivalence toward race mixing and race in general. Using a sample of twenty-four agency websites from the Adoption.com directory, I examined how the language of websites attends to race (see table 3.6). Drawn from a larger sample of public presentations of private agencies on the Internet (see chapter 4), I selected the first eight websites to fit the categories of Color-Blind, Minority or Special Needs programs, and Potentially Color-Blind.

Table 3.5. Adoption Language

Positive/Respectful/Constructive/Honest	Negative/Half-Truth
Adoption triad	Adoption triangle
Adopt from an orphanage	Rescue
Biological parent	Natural/real parent
Biracial	Cross-racial
Birth child	Real child
Birth father/mother	Real/natural mother/father
Birth parent	Real parent
Born to unmarried parents	Illegitimate
Child from abroad	Foreign child
Child placed for adoption	Unwanted or child given away
Child with special needs	Handicapped child
Choosing adoption	Surrender, relinquish
Costs involved in pursuing this adoption	How much you paid for the baby
Court termination	Child taken away
Deciding to parent	Keeping the child/baby
Make an adoption plan/choose adoption	Give away/give up/place
Parent preparation	Home study
Intercountry/international adoption	Foreign adoption
Making contact with	Reunion
My child	Adopted child
Parent	Adoptive parent
Permission to sign a release	Disclosure
Transracial	Cross-racial/mixed-race
Was adopted	Is adopted
Search	Track down parents
To parent	To keep
Unplanned pregnancy	Unwanted pregnancy
Waiting child	Adoptable child/available child

NOTE: This list is an amalgam of variations of Respectful Adoption Language, Unwanted Adoption Language, Adoption-Speak, and Positive Adoption Language.

Table 3.6. Language of Race on Private Agency Websites

Agency Program(s)	Language	Policy
Color-Blind	Explicitly inclusive	One domestic program
Minority or Special Needs	Explicit racial distinctions for adoptive children and programs	Traditional program; more than one minority program
Potentially Color-Blind	Inclusive language but lacking sufficient information to know whether there are separate adoption programs or if all children are included in one domestic program	Inadequate information

Private agencies with color-blind policies typically use inclusive language to describe their programs. Only one of these eight sites includes direct statements about color blindness. Others describe the children in their programs using phrases such as "regardless of race, ethnicity, religion, or special needs" or "Our Domestic Infant Program includes all U.S.-born children that could be full Caucasian, African American, Hispanic, Asian, Native American or any integration of the above." One agency weaves its policy of fairness throughout the site with this statement: "Whether the child or adoptive parent is white, black, Hispanic, or biracial; gentile, Jewish, or nondenominational; special needs or disabled, FCAP realizes the foundation for any adoption is love, caring, and compassion." Private agencies with racial adoption programs use explicit and coded racial referents (e.g., African American/Biracial, Interracial, and Special Needs). Only one website used the term *transracial*. Whether explicit or covert, these programs had a distinctive meaning in private agency websites. "Children are of either full African American heritage or other races and ethnic groups mixed with African American."[7]

Often the ways in which race programs are presented is more striking than their labels. One cannot help but detect the marketing aspect of language used to promote these programs. This marketing can but does not always include a financial aspect. For example, an agency in the Southwest invites adoptive couples to consider getting their Latino infant from the United States: "We have a large number of Hispanic birth mothers, and for families considering traveling to Latin America, this can be a much easier alternative." A few agencies in the Southwest also offer another category of Latino infant—the half-Hispanic/half-Caucasian infant—with a caveat that the child may look fully Hispanic. In another example, Adoptions from the Heart, the implication is that adoptive parents of African American babies can get money back: "Please be aware that there is up to a $10,630 federal tax credit for families. The current placement fee for this program is $9,000." American Adoptions assures the adoptive parent(s), "We do not limit ourselves to advertising in one state. Our national advertising program, combined with our marketing research, allows us to be efficient in locating birth mothers. In fact, we are contacted by over 150 women each month inquiring about our adoption services." Some agencies appeal to a humanitarian or spiritual impulse: "BOC (Babies of Color) Placements are a special opportunity to model God's unconditional love." Another agency offered a deal: : "If you apply with us during January, we will waive the $250 application fee." These statements read like advertising slogans for cars or appliances, where a special feature of the sale must be made to appeal to the consumer.

AGAPE in Nashville, Tennessee simply lists its programs with their adjacent prices: "Special Needs and Healthy Caucasian Infants ($5,000 and $9,500 respectively)." "Special Needs" includes "African-American and biracial infants; those with a physical, mental, or emotional handicapping condition; those age nine (9) or older; or those in a sibling group of three (3) or more." The headline for this program reads, "Special Children Need Special People as Parents." AGAPE's Healthy Caucasian Infant program reads slightly different: "There are very few infants available for adoption who fit this description. Therefore, the Board of Directors sets requirements that applicants must meet for adoption of these children when they are available." Another agency simply combines a sales pitch with its program listings: "For healthy white infants, this fee is 12 percent of the family's previous year's income—$3,000 minimum to $8,000 maximum. African American children—no fee. Special needs children— as low as $300. Can be $0 with board approval."

At one time, advertising children was considered ungainly and unethical. Now advertising by private adoption agencies (and adoptive parents) appears to be standard practice. *New York Times* reporter Laura Mansnerus quotes the president of the California Association of Adoption Agencies as saying, "In this marketplace, it's a sad reality. Luck enters into it, but it's like anything else in life: If you have enough money, you'll get what you think you want. . . . This has left only the thinnest line between buying a child and buying adoption services that lead to a child" (1998, A-16). Mansnerus goes on to say that "scarcity has created a cast of thousands of intermediaries, who can and do sell access to the young women who might relinquish babies . . . [agencies] do what they can to increase their supply of children" (A-16). Clearly, they also do what they can to move their inventory of children.

Potentially color-blind websites fail to provide enough information to know how or whether they deal with transracial or race programs. Adoption language on potentially color-blind websites is inclusive and uses statements similar to color-blind agencies (e.g., "Our agency was founded on the heart-felt belief that all children deserve the best we have to give—love, nurturance and stability." However, sites with race programs (see chapter 4) also have similar mission statements prior to delineating which children can expect placement.

Because of the controversial nature of transracial adoption, many adoption agencies are not open about their transracial adoption policies (NAIC 2004a). Added to the lack of accountability of private agencies, this makes it difficult to assess whether an agency is actually color-blind or color conscious.

Nevertheless, racial language interfaces with policy and practice as these websites display how private adoption agencies subtly shape identities and influence which children are made most attractive to adoptive parents. No doubt advertising also reflects knowledge of the "market" and which children are highly prized by adoptive parents but what questions or images does this language raise in the minds of other adoptive parents and how do these discursive practices construct positive social identities for black or biracial persons?

CONCLUSION

Adoption in the United States presents the paradox of a system governed by race-neutral policy that prohibits considerations of race in adoptive placement yet promotes market mechanisms manifested in the private adoption industry. By law race cannot be factored into placement; yet in private adoption children are categorized, labeled, described, and priced along racial lines. The obviously race-conscious practice of private agencies contradicts this color-blind policy, and on websites of private agencies, private identifiers such as race become public code. No doubt an argument can be made that these racial categories are necessary and represent special attempts to find homes for children. Nevertheless, the racial discourse in private-agency websites is provocative and implicitly evaluative, showing the second-rate status of African Americans and the race-conscious preferences for white infants. Apparently, race matching and race consciousness are only allowed in the "free" market of adoption. One is reminded of Patricia Johnston's statement, "Respectful Adoption Language is a very serious business" (2004, 143).

When it comes to race, the discourse of private adoption represents superficial rather than substantive change as racial categorizations in adoption remain disturbingly real and relatively unchanged from the past. Adoption language demonstrates the insidious and enduring power of racial representations and racial projects, with laws that forbid consideration of race but private adoption programs that attend to it religiously and often surreptitiously. It is commonly understood that the adoption industry has opened its doors to

participants previously refused services. It is also known that some participants are more equal than others. As Dan Savage stated in the *New York Times*
(cited in Fisher 2003, 343), "It is an open secret among social workers that gay
and lesbian couples are often willing to adopt children most heterosexual couples won't touch: H.I.V.-positive children, mixed-race children, disabled children, and children who have been abused or neglected." This is also true for
single adoptive parents.

And while these populations may be more willing to adopt children with
special needs, they are also encouraged by members of the adoption industry
to do so; that is, the market explanation of demand ignores the role of the
adoption industry in directing certain groups of adoptive parents in specific
ways. One example comes from the *Handbook for Single Adoptive Parents*
(Marindin 1992). Informing single adoptive parents about the biases of social
workers in adoption agencies and the preferences of birth mothers, the book
encourages them to be open to adopting special needs children. Another example of how this discourse plays out is found in *The Encyclopedia of Adoption* (Adamec and Pierce 2000), where Native American autonomy over the
placement of their children is framed by saying that Native Americans are "the
only group that continues to be deprived of the protections of MEPA-IEP."
Given the lack of change in racial language, the juxtaposition of categories of
racialized adoptions, the continued use of hypodescent to define and separate
African American and biracial children (i.e., the practice of assigning the socially subordinate status of black to a mixed race child, which in its extreme
form, took the practice of the "one-drop" rule to define black), and the implicit assumptions underlying these practices, it is clear that changed demographics and market forces are just as consequential for changes in adoption
discourse as enlightenment of the adoption industry or America.

What is needed is a counterdiscourse that challenges false presentations of
race and new structures that challenge racist practices. Those who recognize
the social gravity of racism in private adoption must walk the fine line of
shaping a new racial discourse that surpasses the limits of the current language in adoption regarding race. At the same time, we must remain aware of
the political and social implications of these categories in order to transform
the racial logic of our culture. As James Davis suggests, it is possible that the
only way the issue of hypodescent or the "one-drop rule" will be eliminated is
if its parent social construction—"race itself—declines in importance"

(1991). Currently, the language of private adoption reflects the larger color-conscious society in which it operates.

NOTES

1. *Racial formation* is defined by Omi and Winant (1994) as the social and historical processes by which racial categories are created, occupied, and transformed.

2. "Racial project" comes from Michael Omi and Howard Winant's *Racial Formation in the United States: From the 1960s to the 1980s* (1994) and refers to examinations of the historical context of race and how it has been used by those in power to rationalize the distribution of wealth and opportunity. This concept is used to denote how the dominant group prescribes racial policies, which adapt the ideology of the dominant group into practice.

3. As a researcher, I approached adoption in much the same way as I approach a research project. After contacting eight Chicago agencies and speaking with a representative from each, my partner and I attended several workshops of two adoption agencies, where I collected flyers, articles, and pamphlets on adoption-related issues, including but not limited to language and transracial adoption. In addition to the three books presented, the list of adoption popular books examined includes the following:

> *Dear Birthmother,* by Kathleeen Silber
> *Adoption and the Schools: Resources for Parents,* by Lansing Wood and Nancy Ng
> *An Educator's Guide to Adoption,* by the Institute for Adoption Information
> *Family Bonds,* by Elizabeth Bartholet
> *Inside Transracial Adoption,* by Gail Steinberg and Beth Hall
> *Black Baby White Hands,* by Jaiya John
> *Weaving a Family,* by Barbara Katz Rothman
> *Adopting after Infertility,* by Patricia Irwin Johnston
> *Twenty Things Adopted Kids Wish Their Adoptive Parents Knew,* by Sherrie Eldridge
> *Talking with Young Children about Adoption,* by Mary Watkins and Susan Fisher

4. Eugenics advocates attributed various qualities to heredity. These include mental ability, physical and mental health, criminality, educability, and sexual morality. Not surprisingly, eugenics discourse also linked temperament and behavior to race.

5. Early adoption laws required matching only by religion. The fact that the South maintained a state of de jure segregation while de facto segregation dominated in the North, and most early adoption agencies refused services to black birth mothers and/or children mitigated the necessity of such laws regarding race matching. Also,

throughout the first eight decades of the twentieth century, "normal" typically referred to white married heterosexual couples that were economically and socially middle class.

6. Simon and Alstein (1977) point to numerous studies from the mid-1950s into the 1970s that reveal the difficulties for black adoptive couples in obtaining a black child. Data gathered from the CWLA (Child Welfare League of America) survey of 240 public and private adoption agencies in 1970 show that for every 116 approved white homes for one hundred white children, there were only 39 approved nonwhite homes per available one hundred nonwhite children. The report concludes that "the reader must be cautioned that the data do not take account the white adoptive homes that are in fact available for the placement of nonwhite children. If it were *possible* to place a nonwhite child in about one out of every nine approved white homes, there would be an available adoption resource for all children reported by the 240 agencies." This statement was issued well before the NABSW's formal protest to transracial adoption, suggesting that the normative structure of adoption was not to consider placement of nonwhite children with white families. It also helps to explain the excess of nonwhite children who remained unadopted in institutional settings. Simon and Alstein also provide evidence to suggest a relationship between the number of black social workers in an agency and the degree to which these agencies serve black children and the black community.

7. In much of the adoption literature, the term *transracial* is inclusive of international adoptions by white couples of Asian or Latin American infants and children. Their estimates of numbers of transracial adoptions therefore include these types of adoption. However, other sources (including the private agency websites) use the term *transracial* to refer only to black/white adoptions or black mixed with any other ethnic group. The vacillations and variations regarding which groups get included or excluded with the use of the term prompts the question, Is black the only major racial category remaining?

Race Practice: The Dynamics of Race in Private Adoption

This chapter relies on secondary sources and content analyses of two online adoption directories (one performed in 2004, another in 2006) to examine the public presentation of adoption policies, practices, and language and determine the contradictions or congruence between a claim of color blindness and actual adoption practices. As others have noted, private adoption operates as a marketplace in which both supply and demand shape practices. Analyzing these practices provides insight into whether or not we are becoming a more color-blind nation or whether claiming color blindness is merely a way to maintain white privilege by denying racial inequality, as suggested by Gallagher (2003, 3).

DATA SOURCES

I draw upon information from government agencies and private foundations such as the Alan Guttmacher Institute, the Evan B. Donaldson Adoption Institute, ChildTrends, the National Adoption Information Clearinghouse, the North American Council for Adoptive Children, and the U.S. State Department. These are some of the best sources of adoption information, research, and education, and have been influential in helping to shape adoption and child welfare policy. I also perform a content analysis of private infant adoption agency websites in two online directories, the Open Directory Project (January 10, 2004–January 16, 2004) and the Adoption.com directory (January 2004–August 2006).

Focusing on private adoption agency websites does present some challenges. Because there is no national or public regulatory agency oversight on
private adoption agencies, identifying the total population of private adoption
agencies is virtually impossible. Once they meet requirements for state licens-
ing, no state, federal government, or private organization is responsible for
monitoring private agency practices. It is therefore impossible to have a random or representative sample of all private adoption agencies. I used several
strategies to identify and acquire information from a substantial number of
agencies from different regions of the country listed in online directories, regardless of whether they maintain websites. I examined websites for the design
of each adoption program, for explicit pricing schemes and adoption requirements, and for the language the agencies use to describe their policies. Given
the dynamic nature of directories and websites, there is no way of assuring
that a current analysis of the websites in these directories would conform to
the original analyses. Nevertheless, the general patterns found in the analyses
(performed two years apart) should correspond to any subsequent website
analysis.

WEBSITE SEARCHES
Three types of website searches were used to identify agencies (see table 4.1).
The first search was an open and general search of "private adoption agencies"
done at random and unsystematically. While examining the details of different agencies' programs during this first search, I discovered that a number of
agencies had separate minority infant programs. A second limited search focused specifically on "infant minority adoption programs" as well as "minority adoption programs" and "biracial adoption programs." This search
revealed twenty-two agencies with programs listed under one of these head-
ings and led to the discovery of other terms (e.g., *Diversity* and *Special Needs*)
used by agencies to describe programs in which minority infants are frequently placed. In order to assess how wide-ranging these programs were, I
conducted a third more systematic and comprehensive search in which every
adoption agency listed in the online Open Directory Project was examined.

THE OPEN DIRECTORY PROJECT (DMOZ.ORG)
The Open Directory Project (DMOZ) is advertised as the "largest, comprehensive human-edited directory of the Web" and is constructed and main-

Table 4.1.   Web Page Search Strategy

1. Open, general, and unsystematic examination of private adoption agencies
2. Specific search for "minority adoption programs"
3. Systematic examination of all agencies listed in the Open Directory Project (dmoz.org):
   274 = Total number of adoption agencies
   122 = Agencies focused exclusively on international adoptions
   24 = Public agencies or state systems of foster care and adoption
   8 = "No web page can be found"
   8 = Little to no information provided (e.g., main page just lists contact information with no further links)
   10 = Noninfant (i.e, teens or older children), home studies, or referrals only

   96 = Private domestic adoption agencies (39 percent with minority programs: 13 *explicit* and 25 *nonexplicit*)

Note: The 13 explicit programs were also found in the second search on "minority adoption programs"; therefore, combining searches 2 and 3, a total of 47 private adoption agency websites were examined where minority programs are listed somewhere (22 explicit, 25 nonexplicit).

tained by a global community of volunteer editors. Obviously, there are many different online directories. I focused on the DMOZ because it lists a large number of agencies, and I had no reason to assume that it lists any one kind of agency more than others. This was one way to identify a specific set of agency websites that could be systematically examined to get a sense of the extent of practices identified using the first two strategies. The DMOZ listed 274 adoption agencies. Of the 274 listed agencies, 128 focused exclusively on international adoption and 24 involved public agencies or state systems of foster care and adoption. These were eliminated from further consideration because of the interest in private infant domestic agencies. Of the remaining 122 adoption agencies, 8 did not have active websites, 8 provided little to no information about any type of adoption programs, 6 were domestic agencies based in other countries (such as England or Canada), and 10 involved either noninfant adoption (teens and older children) or were not full-service agencies (providing home studies and referrals only). This left a total of 96 private, U.S.-based adoption agency websites to study.

These ninety-six private adoption agencies' programs were explored in detail. Every web page and drop-down menu on each website was examined. I identified three kinds of agencies: those that had explicitly advertised minority adoption programs on their websites (*Explicit* = 13); those that did not overtly advertise minority programs on their websites but maintained separate programs by race or ethnicity (*Nonexplicit* = 25); and those that provided no information regarding race in their programs (*Potentially Color-Blind* = 58).[1] This search revealed that over a third, or approximately four in ten (39 percent), of the private adoption agencies in the DMOZ maintained minority programs. Because the thirteen *explicit* minority programs found in this search were also found in the prior Web search for "minority programs," a total of forty-seven minority adoption programs were identified through the different search strategies (twenty-two explicit and twenty-five nonexplicit).

For the *nonexplicit* minority programs, information regarding the separation of minority infants into separate adoption programs was buried in the websites, found only in the fee structure and/or the application drop-down menus. (Not all sites offer this information; most of the ninety-six sites, particularly the fifty-eight *potentially color-blind* agencies, simply have a "Contact Us" drop-down menu.) In one case, this information was under Frequently Asked Questions ("FAQ" drop-down menu), with the agency responding to a question about gender selection of the infant and including information on "our Caucasian adoption program." Thus, the information was often acquired only when the program was examined in depth and occasionally only inadvertently, or when the application for adoption (when an application was offered online) was viewed. Therefore, when every drop-down menu of the ninety-six private agencies was viewed, twenty-five agencies were found to have nonexplicit minority programs that were not obvious initially and required some investigation to locate. The agencies with minority programs in both categories (explicit and nonexplicit) were found in all regions of the country.

It is impossible to state unequivocally whether the fifty-eight remaining potentially color-blind agencies had truly color-blind policies, handled only white babies, or had separate, nonexplicit minority programs that were only available once personal contact was established. However, there are indications that the reality was the latter. First, of the many agencies that did have minority programs, these programs were only identified after going several layers into the website. Often, only after getting to the application stage was it clear that there were separate programs for minority infants. The agencies with nonexplicit minority programs had general language very similar to the potentially color-blind agencies. What seems to distinguish them is the amount of information available on the potentially color-blind agency websites. These agencies provided less information about programs in general and typically asked interested parties to contact them directly for more information. It could be true that potentially color-blind agencies that do not have specific information about race on their websites actually were color-blind (e.g., the agency recruits birth mothers of all races without tracking or providing information about either birth parent's race, and the agency places all infant children in the same program, regardless of race and without variations in requirements or costs). Other indicators suggest that it is more likely that such agencies either very seldom worked with nonwhite birth mothers (and therefore did not need separate programs to handle such adoptions) or that they just provided limited information about minority adoptions on their websites. According to one private-agency social worker who offered advice to adoptive parents on the Internet, stories of African American birth mothers being repeatedly turned away from agencies where they sought to place their children are not uncommon. "Such calls are not unusual at agencies who have a reputation for serving all children. . . . When that 'I am sorry . . .' line is given, it usually means that the agency has never tried very hard to recruit families for minority children, or that when they did the agency was asking too high a fee for the family to accept. This issue is the soft underbelly of the adoption industry in America."

ADOPTION.COM

Subsequent to the analysis, I discovered possible limitations to the DMOZ as a universal subject guide. Originally known as the Netscape Open Directory, the DMOZ was developed to cope with the Internet's incredible rate of growth by having volunteer editors for each subject category. Problematic to research are the potential personal or political biases of editors directing viewers to related subjects or links (Ó Dochartaigh 2002).[2] I therefore decided to perform a similar analysis on another directory, Adoption.com, which claimed to be one of the three largest adoption directories on the Internet, listing 1,552 adoption agencies and service providers (see table 4.2). This directory was also examined systematically to assess whether the practices found in the DMOZ were simply an artifact of that directory. Many of the agencies in the DMOZ were also listed in the Adoption.com directory. The size of Adoption.com's directory (five times the size of the DMOZ) allows us to assume that the agencies in Adoption.com extended beyond those found in the DMOZ.

Of 1,552 agencies listed in the Adoption.com directory, 196 focused exclusively on international adoption, and 377 involved public agencies or state systems of foster care and adoption. After eliminating these agencies, I found that
142 agencies did not have active websites; 266 provided little to no information about any type of adoption programs (often with only a picture, their title, address, and telephone number); 69 involved either noninfant adoption
(teens and older children), home studies, or referrals only; 7 were lawyers; and
52 were not full-service adoption agencies. Included in the Adoption.com directory were 35 dedicated private agencies that focused exclusively on either
special-needs adoptions (defined as severe social or physical disabilities), or
African American or Native American adoptions of infants and children (e.g.,
Binogii Placement Agency, The African American Adoption Project). I also
found 31 agencies had been duplicated in the directory. This was particularly
true for Catholic Charities agencies but included other agencies as well. Again,
because my focus was on private-agency infant adoption, I was left with a total of 377 U.S.-based private adoption agency websites to examine.

Each of the 377 remaining agency websites was explored in detail. In this
directory, 73 agencies explicitly advertised minority adoption programs on
their websites (*Explicit* = 73), and 53 did not advertise minority programs but
maintained separate programs by race or ethnicity (*Nonexplicit* = 53). Thus, a
total of 126 minority adoption programs were identified in this search. Distinctive in Adoption.com were 36 websites with explicitly color-blind policies
regarding placement of infants and children (e.g., *Adoption of Babies and
Children, Inc., Childplace Inc.). In these programs, children were described as
coming from different racial and ethnic backgrounds, but they were not separated into different programs, and fee schedules were typically sliding scales
based on net worth or annual income. One agency, First Coast Adoption Professionals, called itself "A Colorblind Agency of Caring" and stated its policy
of assistance and compassion toward both adoptive parents and children. The
remaining 251 agencies provided no information regarding race in their programs (*Potentially Color-Blind* = 251).

Analysis of the private infant domestic agencies in Adoption.com revealed
similar patterns to the analysis of the DMOZ, with a third of private infant
adoption agencies (33 percent) maintaining minority programs. What was
different in this directory was the larger number of explicit relative to *nonexplicit* programs (seventy-three versus fifty-three). As in the first directory, the

Table 4.2. Adoption.com Directory Search

1552 = Total number of adoption agencies
 196 = Agencies focused exclusively on international adoptions
 377 = Public agencies or state systems of foster care and adoption
 142 = "No web page can be found"
 266 = Little to no information provided
  69 = Noninfant (i.e., teens or older children), home studies, or referrals only
   7 = Lawyers
  52 = Not adoption agencies (usually part of a network of social service agencies for
       families)
  31 = Agencies found more than once in the directory
  35 = Dedicated private agencies focusing on either special needs (severe social or
       physical disabilities), or Native American or African American adoptions of infants
       and children (e.g., Binogii Placement Agency or The African American Adoption
       Project)

 377 = Private domestic adoption agencies (33 percent minority programs: 73 *explicit* and
       53 *nonexplicit*)

nonexplicit programs had to be found by looking at each of the drop-down menus and exploring the site in depth. While the percentages differ from the first website search (33 percent compared to 39 percent in the DMOZ), the number of agencies supporting separate programs was still a third of all private infant agencies in the directory.

Another interesting feature of this directory was the variation among religiously affiliated agencies, of which Catholic Charities (CC) made up the largest share. These agencies showed substantial variation in policy (fee schedules were typically not provided). For example, a Midwest CC agency maintained separate programs that included "Caucasians," "Minority," and "International" adoptions, while a CC agency in Connecticut made no distinctions between programs. A CC agency in Southern California required acceptance of diversity, stating that the adoptive child would necessarily be at least one-fourth racially different from the adoptive parents. Marital status and sexual orientation were also treated differently between CC agencies, occasionally deviating from official church doctrine. A California agency required religious affiliation of at least one adoptive parent (as part of a heterosexual married couple) and that the parent be a practicing Roman Catholic, while a New York agency stated its openness to all couples, singles, and "differing lifestyles," with any or no particular religious affiliation accepted.

More research is needed to assess the agency practices and policies of the 215 *potentially color-blind agencies*. Perhaps naming and sorting by race was

not seen as necessary by these agencies. The lack of attention to race and ethnicity may reflect a genuine shift in thinking about these social constructions.
Possibly, some agencies downplayed racial programs in an effort to avoid con-
troversies surrounding them. Some may have failed to promote transracial
adoption programs but still maintained them. Others may have dealt with
transracial adoption on a case-by-case basis, upon contact with adoptive parents. In these situations, race need not have been mentioned at all or only in
coded references. For example, though listing a minority program, the Family
Service of Westchester did not include a racial referent for its "Traditional"
program and instead suggested "for those who are seeking to adopt healthy infants. As you may know, nationally, this population of infants is in the greatest demand." In this case, the term *healthy* can be interpreted as a code for
white or Caucasian, as race was never mentioned. It was assumed that the
reader would understand the implicit meaning of *traditional*. Other agencies
did not claim separate race programs but also used the descriptors *traditional,*
Caucasian, or *healthy* in the title of their adoption programs, leaving us to
speculate about their other practices and programs. It is also possible that the
policies and practices of potentially color-blind agencies reflect a neoliberal
racial ideology making its way into private adoption, where whiteness continues to act as the unacknowledged marker against which all other groups are
measured. Here words like *healthy* and *traditional* become metaphors for
white, a fact that remains invisible and therefore is all the more insidious.

As suggested earlier, because websites provide public representations of
agency practices, they offer a window into adoption policy. Beyond issues of
social acceptability, agencies advertise and compete with each other for a
limited population of adoptive clients. Presumably, these factors lead agencies
to present themselves in the best possible way, whether that is approached
by highlighting or masking separate race-based adoption programs. What is
clear is that a significant number of agencies (126 of 377) engage in both
types of practices, with the possibility that these numbers are even larger
than is evident.

CHANGES IN PATTERNS AND MARKET FORCES OF ADOPTION

In order to understand the changing face of private adoption, it is important
to look at the market forces that generate current adoption practices. For a variety of social, economic, and demographic reasons, many Americans look to

adoption as a means of building their families. More and more persons/couples are delaying childbirth or experiencing infertility, and more single persons and same-sex couples are seeking to build families through adoption. Increased diversity of family forms is matched by other cultural and demographic changes to underscore both interest in and problems with adoption. These include the legalization of abortion, increased availability and use of contraceptives, and increased acceptance of single and/or teen parenting (Abma et al. 1997; Chandra et al. 1999; Bacharach, London, and Maza 1991; NCHS 1997; Hollingsworth 1998; McRoy 1989; Alexander and Curtis 1996). However, the demand, estimated as a "ratio of approximately six adoption seekers for every actual adoption," applies mostly to white newborns and infants, not necessarily to children of color (Freundlich 2000a, 9). The percentage of infants placed for adoption who were white declined from 19.3 prior to 1973 to 1.7 in 1995, according to the National Center for Health Statistics (NCHS 1997). Freundlich suggests that the imbalance between supply and demand has increased not only the costs of adoption but also the interest in looking elsewhere for newborns (i.e., international adoption).

DEMAND-SIDE DYNAMICS

Before looking at the purveyors of adoption services and in order to understand how U.S. infants of color fare in this market, it is necessary to look at which group(s) represents the demand side of the adoption equation. Quite simply, which children get adopted is largely a function of who is doing the adopting. The demographic trends offered earlier are only part of the adoption picture, with the different histories, institutional practices, and societal expectations surrounding children of different races and ethnicities providing the backdrop.

Traditional practices described in chapter 3 (e.g., the historic refusal of many, if not most, adoption agencies to serve communities of color until midway through the twentieth century and the enduring policies of race matching that prevailed throughout this time) combine with laws, cultural differences, and financial costs to render adoption, specifically private infant adoption, a predominantly white middle- and upper-middle-class enterprise. (For more information on the history of the changing definitions, see Zeliger [1985] and Wegar [1997].) These may be the most significant factors driving the political economy of racism in adoption as the demand by white adoptive parents has resulted in a market where economic and political forces related to race continue to dominate (Chandra et al. 1999; Alexander and Curtis 1996).

One of the most significant factors involved in who adopts is the financial cost of adoption. Although the illegal exchange of money in adoption is forbidden by law (i.e., one cannot technically buy a baby or a child), adoption laws vary significantly from state to state, and private adoption remains a largely unregulated industry (Zeliger 1985; Freundlich 2000a; Modell 2002). The courts rarely scrutinize adoption expenses charged by private agencies or adoption lawyers. In international adoption, the exchange of money in the form of bribes, albeit illegal, is widely practiced and rarely prosecuted. The fees of private and independent domestic adoptions can range from $4,000 to more than $40,000 and include travel, acquisition of documentation, and the operating costs of an agency (e.g., advertising to solicit birth mothers or services such as medical care provided for birth mothers [NAIC 2003]). A breakdown of estimated costs is provided in table 4.3.

The fees that adoptive parents are assessed essentially pay for the services provided to birth mothers, including those who decide not to place their children for adoption (an estimated 80 percent) as well as the remaining 20 percent who do place their children (Mansnerus 1998).[3] Agencies vary in their disclosure of how funds are spent; however, they typically provide a breakdown of expenses, either formally or informally.[4] Whether prospective adoptive parents are made aware that some of their money may be spent for services unrelated to their particular adoption are issues outside the scope of this book. Still, we can assume that adoptive parents are made aware of an

Table 4.3.   Estimated Operating Costs for Private Agencies

25 percent—Birth-mother services
 6 percent—Locating birth father
10 percent—Home studies
 8 percent—Travel and living expenses
 8 percent—Legal fees
13 percent—Advertising and marketing to find birth parents
13 percent—Fees that support other adoptive parents who adopt children with special
          needs
17 percent—Administrative overhead and salaries of professionals

100 percent

Source: A. Pertman, as cited in Freundlich (2000a)

agency's different adoption programs; therefore, the market value of infants and children, at some level, reflects adoptive parents' willingness to pay the price in order to get their desired "product."

The continued preference for white infants and the rise in intercountry adoptions may be partially due to black opposition to transracial adoption in the United States. Some adoptive persons/couples may be averse to adopting African American children out of sensitivity to the assumed opposition of the African American community, and other adoptive parents may question their ability to adequately parent African American children. The generality of such a concern is doubtful, however, as it assumes that white adoptive parents possess an awareness of and responsiveness to the sentiments of minority communities that is not evident in other arenas of public opinion.

Recent studies also suggest inconsistencies in the attitudes of Americans toward adoption. While the majority of Americans approve of "traditional" and transracial adoption (though this varies significantly by age and sex of survey respondents), adoption practices are quite different. The National Survey of Family Growth (as cited in Chandra, Abma, Maza, and Bachrach 1999) found that of nearly 10 million women who had considered adoption, less than 500,000 actually adopted (Hollingsworth 2000; Princeton Survey Research Associates 1997). Other inconsistencies show up in the National Adoption Attitudes Survey (Harris Interactive 2002), where despite a positive attitude toward adoption (94 percent of adults held favorable or somewhat favorable attitudes toward adoption), over a third of the 1,416 Americans polled held negative beliefs about adopted children (e.g., not as emotionally healthy as biological children; more likely to have behavioral, drug, and alcohol problems). Superimpose upon these more general beliefs the enduring notions regarding race, and it is difficult to believe that empathy is what directs the majority of white American adoptive parents away from transracial adoption.

An argument of cultural or physical similarity is also why some families prefer to adopt white infants: they hope that these children will blend better into their families, at least phenotypically. Another possible reason is the desire of white adoptive persons/couples to avoid open adoption, which promotes ongoing contact between birth parents and adopted children. Given the prevailing wisdom of maintaining contact with birth parents for the emotional well-being of adopted children, the notion that such a policy sends adoptive parents running to other countries in order to avoid it should give us pause. In addition, whether concerns regarding open adoption are coupled with considerations of transracial adoption is not clear. Issues of cultural and physical similarity do not appear to matter with international adoptions—China, Guatemala, and South Korea are three of the top five sending countries for the past ten years (see table 4.4). However, adoptions from some culturally dissimilar countries are embraced much more readily than others, such as from Jamaica or Haiti, where cost and wait times are significantly lower and location is proximal.

There is no doubt that today U.S. private, independent domestic, and intercountry adoptions are a global enterprise reflecting the preferences of the adopting population (Modell 2002). International adoptions have increased dramatically since the mid-1990s, with a majority of children coming from China, Russia, S. Korea, Guatemala, and the Ukraine (U.S. Department of State 2005). The costs of international adoption have increased substantially; so, too, have the number of private agencies handling them, particularly in Russia and Eastern Europe. According to Freundlich (2000a, 43), "The growing number of agency programs in these countries and others has led to increased competition and the need for each agency to position itself as able to provide the most desirable children in the most expeditious manner—for higher fees."

In the year 2000, almost 20,000 children were adopted from other countries (U.S. State Department 2005a). At the same time, nearly 125,000 U.S. children, mostly African American and biracial, remained in need of adoptive homes. This group of children comprises what adoption professionals often refer to as special needs, less likely to be adopted, or the hard to place—codes for older and minority. While recent information from the Evan B. Donaldson

Table 4.4.   Top Five Source Countries for International Adoptions (1995–2005)

FY 2005	China 7,906	Russia 4,639	Guatemala 3,783	South Korea 1,630	Ukraine 821
FY 2004	China 7,044	Russia 5,865	Guatemala 3,264	South Korea 1,716	Kazakhstan 826
FY 2003	China 6,859	Russia 4,939	Guatemala 2,328	South Korea 1,790	Kazakhstan 825
FY 2002	China 5,053	Russia 4,939	Guatemala 2,219	South Korea 1,770	Ukraine 1,106
FY 2001	China 4,681	Russia 4,279	South Korea 1,870	Guatemala 1,609	Ukraine 1,246
FY 2000	China 5,053	Russia 4,269	South Korea 1,794	Guatemala 1,518	Romania 1,122
FY 1999	Russia 4,348	China 4,101	South Korea 2,008	Guatemala 1,002	Romania 895
FY 1998	Russia 4,491	China 4,206	South Korea 1,829	Guatemala 911	Vietnam 603
FY 1997	Russia 3,816	China 3,597	South Korea 1,654	Romania 555	Guatemala 427
FY 1996	China 3,333	Russia 2,454	South Korea 1,516	Romania 555	Guatemala 427
FY 1995	China 2,130	Russia 1,896	South Korea 1,666	Guatemala 449	India 371

Source: U.S. Department of State (2005a).

Adoption Institute (2002) indicates that transracial families are becoming more common, this is predominantly a result of U.S. couples adopting children from Asia and Latin America rather than adopting racial minority children in the United States. The growth in the number of children in foster care since 1987, coupled with the number of foster care children adopted through public agencies, remained low enough that in 1997, the federal government passed the Adoption and Safe Families Act (ASFA) to generate incentives and create mandates for states to substantially increase the adoptions of children in these categories. One of these incentives involved subsidizing adoptions ($4,000 per adoption and $6,000 per special-needs adoption).[5] These federal and state tax credits and subsidies have had some positive effect on the number of foster care adoptions, though there is no data on what effect, if any, they have had on private adoptions.

Despite the passage of ASFA and subsequent improvement in foster care adoptions, in the year 2001, the number of hard-to-place children still in the public system was more than twice the number of children adopted in that year (Adoption and Foster Care Analysis and Reporting System 2002). Hollingsworth (1998) argued that inequities in prevention and intervention services contribute to the disparities between children from different racial/ethnic groups and their successful exit from the child welfare system (e.g., fewer placements and services for families of color than for white families, a surplus of parents seeking white infants and preschool children, and a shortage of those pursuing available children; see also Modell [2002] regarding liberal fiscal policy and its diminishing effects on the distribution of subsidies by states). There are several plausible explanations as to why, once placed in state systems, children tend to remain in them, though length of stay in foster care and the probabilities for adoption also vary significantly by race. It is less clear how minority infants and children are dealt with by private agencies. Because these agencies historically refused to deal with black children, or when they did, they strictly segregated black children, we must ask, In a world in which transracial adoption appears to be on the rise, what are current racial policies and practices of private adoption agencies?

MINORITY CHILDREN IN U.S. PRIVATE ADOPTION AGENCY PROGRAMS

The two searches of private-agency websites found agencies in every region of the country that explicitly provided minority adoption programs. Although

African American infants and children handled by private agencies are generally not assumed to be foster care children mired in state systems (particularly those few programs advertising "healthy African American and biracial infants"), they were placed into distinct adoption programs. Agencies gave different names to these programs: Minority, African American/Biracial, and Special Needs were the most common labels, but titles also included Transracial, Diversity, Babies of Color, and even Challenging Cases. Most had a racial referent of some kind.[6] This was in stark contrast to the seemingly race-neutral names for other programs: Traditional, Domestic, and International.

The language for minority programs is not merely a neutral descriptor; it operates to mark children (most often African American) as the "Other." For example, Adoption Links subdivided its domestic programs into three types, including Infant Minority, but the type of children available to adopt in this program were explicitly described as "African-American babies" with encouragement to families to be open to gender. Catholic Charities of Peoria, Illinois, also divided its adoption programs into several types: Healthy Caucasian Infant, Transracial Adoption (i.e., biracial), Minority Infants (i.e., African American), and International Adoption.

At first glance, Heritage Adoption Services' Diversity Program suggested the possibility of adopting children who were from a variety of ethnic backgrounds. Only upon a closer reading did it become clear that this was a transracial adoption program and that transracial referred specifically and exclusively to the placement of "newborn babies of African-American heritage with families of all ethnicities." Thus, diversity referred to the various ethnic groups *adopting* African American newborns, not to the ethnic diversity of infants. Again, this was not the only program that promoted African American adoption in this manner. Other programs also promoted transracial adoption or the idea that individuals and families of all ethnicities could adopt African American and biracial infants in these programs. The fact that so many programs existed (47 in the first search and 126 in the second) alludes to the possible impact of the 1990s Inter-Ethnic Placement Act as well as the limited effects of black opposition to transracial adoption.

No doubt some would argue that these programs represent the efforts of progressive agencies to promote racial harmony and provide homes for hard-to-place infants. Indeed, agencies might argue for the necessity of highlighting these children for prospective parents by placing them in separate programs. Aside from asking why they would need to do this in a color-blind society, the question remains, How can agencies say they ignore race while so clearly attending to it by creating separate race programs and maintaining language that is both archaic and racially evocative? When descriptors like *healthy* are used to describe one type of child but not another, a flag is implicitly raised in the minds of adoptive parents regarding the other programs without this descriptor. Six agencies in the DMOZ search and twenty-five in Adoption.com used the label *Healthy Caucasian* alongside *Minority, African American*, and/or *Special Needs*. In a color-blind adoption process, adoptive parents (of any race) would work with an agency to adopt an infant (of any race). In the existing market-driven process, the emphasis is on providing options for the predominantly white adoptive parents who are the industry's largest client group.

NONEXPLICIT MINORITY PROGRAMS

Agencies in both searches had minority programs that were unadvertised. In both directories, a number of agencies maintained minority programs that were virtually hidden in the website and located with some difficulty. For example, Adoption Circle included a minority program but did not explicitly advertise this program on either its home page or program page. Beacon House adoption agency began its program descriptions with the heading, "Caucasian Infant Adoption Program." Adoption Associates, Inc., also failed to make race explicit until one tapped into the "Frequently Asked Questions" section of the website, where a description of "our minority and Caucasian adoption programs" was embedded in the answer to a question about choosing the child's gender. At least twenty-five of the agencies in the first search and fifty-three agencies in the second search had adoption programs delineated by race, which would be found only by clients who read every page on the website, particularly the application form.

It was common practice for agencies to promote their philosophy or mission as one in which "we believe that all children deserve a loving family." Only upon examination of the application and/or fees schedule could one find separate adoption programs for white and minority children. Hope for Children adoption agency offered four domestic programs: African American, Caucasian, Hispanic, and Mixed Race. Despite an opening line similar to the one mentioned above, the KidzFirst website directed clients to separate traditional and minority programs after the application and fees sections were read. As many as twenty-five racial/ethnic mixes were listed as "acceptable" for adoptive parents to check in the Traditional program, while eleven racial/ethnic "acceptable" mixes were listed in its Minority program. This agency's allocation of so many different racial/ethnic mixes was idiosyncratic among agencies, but it is clear that folk theories of race, specifically those of the adopting family, were used to separate more or less desirable babies into different programs by other agencies as well.

Even when agencies did not sort adoptions into separate programs on their websites, they could not be assumed to be color-blind (therefore the term *potentially color-blind*). It simply means there was less information on how these agencies dealt with children of color.

CRITERIA FOR ADOPTION

Perhaps even more significant than the language of adoption programs were the different requirements and costs for adopting from minority programs, which varied substantially from traditional and domestic programs. All adoptive programs have requirements that vary, yet clear patterns emerged in requirements for minority programs compared with nonminority programs. Not only did the costs vary by type of adoption program, but also wait time, age requirements, marital status, and family structure allowances. For example, age requirements were more flexible for those adopting from minority programs (i.e., parents could be older, even when adopting infants). More children already present in the home were allowed in minority programs relative to nonminority programs, and marital status was significantly more flexible, with single and "alternative" couples allowed (and often encouraged) to adopt from minority programs. (See the *Handbook for Single Adoptive Parents* [Marindin 1992].)

An examination of agency policies, including eligibility requirements and pricing, suggests that minority programs may represent a niche market, one that is not (or not solely) generated to fill the needs of the African American community but rather a segment of the white adoptive population who either do not want to wait, cannot afford traditional programs, or do not meet the criteria for adopting a white infant. One agency even suggested that the expectations of white birth mothers (regarding allowances for children already in the home) were not an expectation of black birth mothers. Carolina Hope

Christian Adoption Agency told adoptive parents, "If you seek to adopt a Caucasian, healthy infant, then in general, you should be under 50 years old, have
no more than two other children, and not able to have biological children."
However, later in the site, adoptive parents who were open to biracial or
African American infants were told, "Also, birth mothers placing children of
African-American and mixed race heritage are more flexible in the family pro-
file. Often these women do not necessarily seek a couple who only has one or
two children." Regardless of the fact that almost all minority programs maintained different requirements regarding age, children already in the home, and
so forth, the suggestion here was that this particular requirement was not a
function of the adoption industry but rather the result of different expectations of African American birth mothers. Ignored is the likelihood that "flex-
ibility" of African American birth mothers undoubtedly reflects awareness of
limited alternatives combined with the unacknowledged influence of adoption agency workers.

The Evangelical Child and Family Agency (ECFA) stated in its guidelines
for adoption that "childlessness" or infertility was required for "healthy newborn Caucasian, Asian, or Latino adoption" but not required for all others
(i.e., African American). Similar to other agencies, ECFA separated its infants
into five programs: Healthy Newborn Adoption, Special Needs, African-
American Infants, Intercountry Adoption, and Agency-Assisted Adoption.
ECFA also had a marriage requirement of at least two years, with the caveat
that "singles may apply for all forms of adoption except healthy newborn Caucasian, Asian, or Latino adoption (the Healthy Newborn Adoption program);
not required for all others."

If there were some principled and defensible stance that older or nontraditional parents were not acceptable as parents, then these rules would apply to
all potential adoptions. Instead, what appears to be functioning is a market-
driven competition with particular (heteronormative) ideas about "appropriate" family structure, in which young, married heterosexual couples are given
first choice of infants. In this case, demand-side issues (the competition between adopting parents) relegates some adopting families to a less competitive
status (because they are perceived to be nontraditional or "risky") and forces
them to settle for babies that preferred families do not want.

Some agencies promoted their minority programs by acknowledging that
the demand for these children was lower than for others. For example,

Arkansas' Adoption Advantage labeled its program Special Placements: Babies of Color (BOC) and stated, "We offer adoptive parents who participate in the BOC program special financial advantages. Often there is a shortage of parents willing to adopt these children, which means that the wait time is less than with Caucasian adoptions." Unfortunately, Arkansas is not unique in its problems with placing African American and biracial infants. The Love Basket agency also acknowledged, "Children of color and special needs placements are usually completed within one year, as the list of adoptive parents for these children is shorter." The interesting thing about this agency's website is that although the fee schedule represented a sliding scale based on yearly income, infants were still separated into three programs with different sliding scales: Caucasian, Children of Color, and Special Needs, with Children of Color further divided into a Full African American program and Biracial program. No Special Needs program fee schedule was offered. Here, at the level of $100,000-plus annual income of adoptive parents, the fee for a Caucasian infant was $20,000; for a Biracial infant, $16,000; and for a Full African American infant, $9,000.[7] The statement above the fee schedule read, "Thanks to donations we have received, and for the sole purpose of encouraging that couples adopt children of color and special needs children, the agency placement fees are as follows." This statement and others like it suggest that subsidies alone are not the driving force behind private agencies' pricing of children.

The differences in costs of adopting from domestic/traditional versus minority programs were perhaps most striking. A truly color-blind agency would maintain a sliding scale based upon income, without distinctions based on the race of the child. And there are those that do exactly that. While most agencies did not present explicit pricing on their websites, many offered either a statement of reduced fee structure for the minority program or a range of costs for each program. A significant number of agencies did provide the costs of different programs, all of which (except the thirty-six explicitly color-blind agencies) indicated that the average cost of adopting a black child is less than half the fee for a white child (typically between one-third and one-half the price).

One example of the variation between such programs involves the American Adoptions agency with its Traditional I, Traditional II, and Minority programs. The agency made explicit that the traditional programs referred to "the adoption of all non–African American (i.e., Caucasian, Hispanic, Asian, Native American, etc. or any non–African American combination of races) healthy newborns and infants." The Minority program referred to "the adoption of African American (or any race combination with African American heritage) healthy newborns and infants."

The average wait time for the Traditional I program was nine to eighteen months, whereas the average wait time for adopting from the Minority program was one to nine months. Adoptive parents of African American infants could be up to ten years older than those adopting non–African American infants. And while the number of children already present in the adoptive home could not exceed two for either of the traditional programs, there was no limit to the number of children already present in the homes into which African American infants could go. Finally, and perhaps most compelling, was the financial cost of adopting from either of the traditional programs ($20,000–$25,000 for program I and $28,000–$35,000 for program II) compared to that of the Minority program ($10,000–$17,000).

Another example comes from the Adoption Support Center, which had three adoption plans: a domestic adoption involving Caucasian or Hispanic infants; international adoptions; and full and/or biracial African American adoptions. For the domestic Caucasian/Hispanic plan, the average wait time was ten months and the plan was cited as "well suited for couples from 25 to 40 years of age." In contrast, the third plan (African American or biracial adoptions) had a wait time of only three months and was "well suited for single women and couples from 25 to 52 years of age." The minimum costs for the first plan were similar to the quoted maximums for the third. The implicit competition between parents for particular babies was also evident in the guidelines. For example, the website advised that single parents could be considered for "full" Hispanic placements (apparently not at all for Caucasian babies), but they would be at a "disadvantage with *couples*, as most are willing to consider full Hispanic babies as well" (emphasis added). Assumptions about appropriate family structure here intersect with clear preference ordering on the part of adoptive parents to render some much more competitive for the most prized infants. The rank ordering of ethnic preferences was also apparent, with Caucasian babies on the top followed by mixed or full Hispanics and then biracial or fully African American babies. For example, single parents were informed that African American/biracial adoptions were "a very simple and quick route for you" and that prospective parents could, in fact, specify whether they desired "a full or biracial infant." The website included additional explicit language about the race of the babies in the description for the international program: "the ethnic blend of the child is a part of your choice … five international programs offer Caucasian babies" (see table 4.5).

Table 4.5.   Comparative Requirements and Costs of Private Programs

A. Costs

Agency	Range or Total Cost		Placement Fee	
	Domestic	Minority	Domestic	Minority
American Adoptions	$20,000–$25,000	$10,000–$17,000		
Love Basket	$12,390–$20,390	$5,390–$9,390	$7,500–$15,500	$3,500–$7,500
Adoption Links	Not listed	$9,600–$15,500		
Sunny Ridge	$19,500	$7,250	$16,000	$3,500
Heritage	$18,000–$22,000	$7,500–$12,000		

B. Examples of Costs Breakdown
Sunny Ridge (www.sunnyridge.org)

Fees	Domestic Adoption	African American Adoptions
Application	$250	$250
At beginning of adoption preparation	$500	$500
At completion of series of preparations	$3,000	$3,000
Placement	$16,000	$3,500
Total	$19,550	$7,250

Adoption Access, Inc. (www.adoptionaccess.com)

Fees	Caucasian/Caucasian/Hispanic	Fully Hispanic	African American/Biracial
Application	$1600	$1600	$1600
Placement	$30,800–$32,800	$23,800	$12,000–$15,000
Est. finalization	$600	$600	$600
Total	$33,000–$35,000	$26,000	$14,200–$17,200

Plan Loving (www.planlovingadoptions.com)
Minority Infant Adoption Program, fees for Oregon families

Application	$ 300
Communications Fee	$ 100
Coordination Fee	$1100
Program Development Fee	$ 350
Preadopt Classes	$ 150
Adoption Homestudy	$ 850
Post-Placement	$ 550
Court Report	$ 150
Total	$3550

Love Basket (www.lovebasket.org)

Caucasian		Children of Color/Special Needs			
		Biracial		Full African American	
Income	Placement Fee	Income	Placement Fee	Income	Placement Fee
< $40,000	$12,000	< $40,000	$8,000	< $60,000	$5,000
$40,001–$60,000	$14,000	$40,001–$60,000	$10,000	$60,001–$100,000	$7,000
$60,001–$80,000	$16,000	$60,001–$80,000	$12,000	$100,000+	$9,000
$80,001–$100,000	$18,000	$80,001–$100,000	$14,000		
$100,000+	$20,000	$100,000+	$16,000		

C. Example of Requirements
American Adoptions (www.americanadoptions.com)

	Traditional Program I	Traditional Program II	Minority Program
Available Infants	All non–African American healthy newborns and infants (Caucasian, Hispanic, Asian, Native American, or any non–African American combination of races)	All non–African American healthy newborns and infants (Caucasian, Hispanic, Asian, Native American, or any non–African American combination of races)	African American or any combination of African American with any non–African American race
Wait Time	nine–eighteen months	three–nine months	one–nine months
Eligibility Requirements	Couples only; married a minimum of two years; twenty-five–forty-five years old; no more than one child	Couples only; twenty-five–fifty years old; no more than two children	twenty-five–fifty-five years old; number of children may vary
Fees	$20,000–$25,000	$28,000–$35,000	$10,000–$17,000

Even in an agency whose program focused solely on African American and Latino infants (i.e., Plan Loving Adoption's Minority Infant program), the upper limit of the range of placement fees for African American infants was the lower limit of the placement fees for Latino infants.[8] The prices of adoption agencies with minority programs revealed a tremendous discrepancy in adoption placement fees that even government or state subsidies would be unlikely to nullify.

These websites raise questions regarding money, race, and the ethics of adoption. Why is there such a range of private agency fees, and why do the fees and requirements vary so significantly by the race/ethnicity of the child? If lower costs for minority programs are truly designed to help African American families adopt, why the accompanying age, marital status, and family structure differences, and why are so many of these programs buried in an agency's website? Are we really trying to provide opportunities for other groups to adopt, or are we allowing children to be commodified by a market that values some children more than others? If prices truly reflect demand and adoption representatives acknowledge their inability to solicit adoptive parents at higher prices, then clearly, color blindness is far from a reality.

ADOPTION AND THE LATIN-AMERICANIZATION OF RACE IN THE UNITED STATES

Another interesting feature of the website examination is that not all minority children were sorted into minority or diversity programs. In fact, apart from Plan Loving and the Spence-Chapin Foundation, which had separate African American and Latino adoption programs, no other private agencies in the DMOZ or the Adoption.com directory placed Latino or Asian infants into minority programs. Most agencies included Asians and Hispanics in domestic or traditional programs, excluding only African Americans. When an agency had a minority program, it specifically targeted African Americans. Indeed, reminiscent of the one-drop rule, a mix of any ethnic group and African American designated the child as biracial and subsequently located him or her in the African American or minority program. No other racial or ethnic mixes were so labeled. Other mixed-race children (e.g., Asian American and white or Latino and white) were not categorized as biracial, and when separated from traditional or Caucasian programs, often occupied a middle category. In fact, in some programs, a mix of either Hispanic or Asian parentage with white shifted the infant or child into the Caucasian or traditional category (upward mobility, if you will). Similarly, the price (and other requirements) also shifted upward to that of a Caucasian, or white, infant. However, a child of African American and white parents was subject to the rule of hypodescent and placed into the minority program. These placements are centrally about who will take what kind of infant and tied in closely with folk theories of race. It is not at all clear that an Asian American baby blends in better with a white family than an African American baby, but adoptive parents' preferences for some children over others facilitates their willingness to pay more, wait longer, and take on additional potential risk to get their preferred child.

The private adoption industry does not simply reflect these preferences; it also facilitates them by locating infants and children along a racial continuum upon which race and ethnicity and particular racial/ethnic mixes have implications for the costs and requirements of adoption. In this way, private adoption agencies illustrate a rare (in terms of its explicitness) way in which the meanings of race are rather plainly laid out. Such adoptive programs and their use of language (e.g., Caucasian, Special Needs) represent dated racial thinking along with guidelines that are hard to reconcile with current claims of color blindness. Another phenomenon that calls into question claims of color blindness is international adoption.

INTERNATIONAL ADOPTION:
THE ALTERNATIVE TO MINORITY PROGRAMS?

In the past twelve years, the rates of international adoption have tripled. As the doors to Russia and countries previously part of the Soviet Union have opened, adoption from these countries has increased dramatically (Evan B. Donaldson Adoption Institute 2002). Undoubtedly, the rate of adoption from foreign countries has much to do with different countries' policies, restrictions, fees, and availability of children. Nevertheless, in a color-blind society, race would be eliminated as a factor influencing the market, leaving other factors—such as cost, wait time, travel, and so forth—responsible. The difference between costs of even the low end of an international adoption compared to a U.S. minority program adoption should translate into greater interest in the latter. Most arguments about adoption include a market-driven rationale, so why do U.S. citizens incur the added costs involved in international adoption when there are minority programs with reduced fees, shorter wait time, and fewer restrictions, not to mention the lack of comparatively significant travel expenses?

There are also the hidden risks of international adoption as highlighted in newspaper articles, State Department bulletins, international organizations such as UNICEF (United Nations Children's Fund), and even private-agency orientations and seminars. These include mental and emotional problems of infants and children stemming from institutionalization (ranging from delayed cognitive and emotional development to schizophrenia) as well as substance abuse issues (fetal alcohol syndrome) and pediatric AIDS.[9] For those familiar with the process of adoption, added complexities of crossing international borders, paperwork, and negotiation of a child's life without optimal access to information generate even greater risks for adoptive families and raise serious questions as to why a quarter of all U.S. international adoptions come from China, and why rates of adoption from Russia and the Ukraine have increased rapidly. Given that agencies advertise the latter two as good options for securing Caucasian children, it seems that prospective parents are willing to take on considerable cost and risk to adopt babies of a particular hue.

Just as the U.S. private domestic adoption arena reveals a racial/ethnic preference ordering, the U.S. international adoption market also reflects the latinization of the United States described by Bonilla-Silva (2001, 2003), with the top five sending countries over the past ten years being China, Russia, South Korea, Guatemala, and the Ukraine. Some sociologists suggest that over the decades, Chinese Americans have moved from being "almost black" to "almost white" and are the next immigrant group in line to become white (J. Lee and Bean 2003). This may explain the significant interest in Chinese adoptions, with these children viewed as the model minority and assigned honorary white status. Similarly, the dramatic increases in adoption from Russia (and the former Soviet republics) may also reflect the pigmentocracy described earlier, in which, despite cultural differences (and the added potential problems involved in these adoptions), the risks and the prices are worth the skin color. At any rate, a look at data on international adoptions over the past twenty years suggests support for Bonilla-Silva's tripartite system of racial categories.

I spoke informally with a few adoption professionals in the Chicago area about the website searches. Having described the patterns found in each of the directories, I asked if they could offer any insights into the results of these searches. Each of the five persons with whom I spoke (a private-agency director, an associate director, a social worker, and two adoption lawyers) maintained that, in their experience, adoptive parents were far from color-blind, gender neutral, or age indifferent.[10] One of the lawyers reported that clients had returned adopted biracial children to him, claiming that they were "darker" and "looked more African American" than expected. The social worker described adoptive parents who acknowledged preferences at the onset of the process by stating, "We'll take anything but a black child." One of the agency directors referred to the headlines made by another agency, whose practice of placing a large number of African American infants with adoptive parents from other countries received national attention (see ABC World News 2005). This director acknowledged that her agency also engaged in the same practice, although with significantly fewer placements. Adoption.com even includes a few websites of agencies declaring their interest in placing African American and biracial infants with either couples or singles who reside in the United States or Canada (e.g., Adoption Star and Adoption Associates, Inc.). Given the dynamic aspects of websites it remains to be seen whether more private agencies will begin targeting Canadians and Europeans as prospective adoptive parents, at least for African American and biracial infants. Obviously, these conversations with adoption professionals are far from conclusive in addressing the issues raised here, but their experiences and perceptions clearly support further investigation into the argument of race as a factor in the demand of infants and children. For those who disagree, a useful exercise would be to answer this question: What would be the response if the infants placed with Canadians and Europeans were white infants born in the United States?

CONCLUSION

This chapter takes a look at the public presentation of private adoption agencies in the United States and how these presentations reflect contradictions with the current political commitment to color blindness. The explicit policies of private adoption agencies (as laid out in public websites) offer one example of the persistent significance of skin color in the United States The labeling of distinct minority adoption programs juxtaposes black babies against "healthy" infants in the "traditional" programs and embodies difference. Such programs set children in minority programs even further outside the mainstream than their parented and nonblack adoptive counterparts. Regardless of the functional, benign, or even altruistic motives claimed by adoption agencies, racial distinctions are perpetuated and the color line protected when African American and biracial children are separated from virtually everyone else in adoption programs. The specific organization of such programs makes it clear that the presumed adoptive family is white and would prefer a traditional, or domestic, baby. In a subtle taken-for-granted way, these distinct programs represent private adoption agencies' exercising of interpretive control, the power to name and to separate some from others, and to claim only the best intentions in doing so. This language and these practices are far from color-blind.

The marginalization of African American infants does not have its origins in private adoption; rather, racial differences exist within a social, economic, and political hierarchy of meaning, complete with the sets of assumptions surrounding race that are embedded in our society and translate to "less than," both figuratively and financially. Nevertheless, the communicative power of these programs perpetuates myths about entire communities and allows identities to be sustained by the color line. It is easy to assume that the separation and low cost of adopting an African American infant is related to something "wrong" with the child, such as suffering from the mother's (supposed) drug abuse or fetal alcohol syndrome. Indeed, a past director of Adoptive Families of America is quoted in the *New York Times* as acknowledging, "I hate to say this because it's going to sound crass, but there are people who have the basic philosophy that the more I pay for something, the better it will be, not just in terms of the product but in terms of appearances. It says a lot about me if I drive a Lexus" (Mansnerus 1998: A16). While it is hard to know whether people regard white infants as a Lexus and black infants as a Ford Escort, this system of adoption fits perfectly with "color-blind" ideology by claiming to ignore racial hierarchy even as it assists in sustaining it, arranging children by race and organizing transracial adoption practices.

The practice of adoption in the United States illustrates the emergence of a new form of color-blind racism in our society that allows whites to argue that race no longer matters even as their adoption practices clearly demonstrate that it does. New color-blind racial ideologies are important precisely because they allow whites to continue to justify the status quo while continuing to engage in many quite race-conscious behaviors (Bonilla-Silva 2001; Doane 2003; Lewis 2001). As Gallagher (2003, 1) put it, "The color-blind perspective removes from personal thought and public discussion any taint or suggestion of white supremacy or white guilt while legitimating the existing social, political, and economic arrangements which privilege whites." Or as Banks (1998, 3) said in reference to adoption practices, "White adoptive parents' racial preferences for white children are emblematic of the race-consciousness that serves as the linchpin of racial inequality."

It may well be true that some whites are hesitant to adopt black children because they are concerned about their ability to provide proper racial socialization, while other whites may be responding to black opposition to transracial adoption by looking elsewhere for their children. However, there is ample evidence that this is not the sole or even primary dynamic at work here. There is clear evidence that Korean children adopted into white families and communities face considerable challenges to their racial identity development (Cox 1999; Kim 2000; Trenka 2003, 2006; R. Lee 2004). This has not impeded interest in adopting Asian babies. Additionally, the passage of laws such as the Multi-Ethnic and Inter-Ethnic Placement Acts, the significant number of minority adoption programs available, and the adoption of U.S. black infants and children by Canadians and Europeans reflect the rather limited impact of black opposition to such activity.

The adoption industry also provides us with an illustration of the changing nature of racial hierarchies in the United States, shifting from a strict white to nonwhite hierarchy to a more Latin American–like structure in which the children of some groups are given honorary white status (and subsequently, white market prices) while others are denied this status. This has made the implementation of minority programs more complicated and represents shifting understandings of race and ethnic relations. However, it does not necessarily indicate the decreasing significance of race generally or in adoption in particular. The examination of private agency websites suggests that the political economy of racism continues to dominate adoption practices, with a preference ordering of infants and children drawn along racial/ethnic lines. Whatever the intentions of those advocating or even declaring the achievement of color blindness in adoption, in this arena "closest to home" we not only remain aware of color but continue to attach great significance to it.

NOTES

I gratefully acknowledge the contribution of Amanda Lewis toward analysis of agencies in the first directory (Open Directory Project), along with her insights on racism in America.

1. These programs are referred to as explicit, nonexplicit, and potentially color-blind so as to be as descriptive as possible. *Explicit* minority programs were unambiguously advertised, prominently displayed, and outlined overtly on either the home page or the adoption program page of the websites. Information about *nonexplicit* minority programs required some effort to locate and was often found fortuitously. Though intentionality cannot be ascribed to this structure (by labeling such programs as "concealed" or "hidden"), it is noteworthy that many of these nonexplicit programs were described by agencies that have used color-blind discourse on front pages in describing their work. The third category, *potentially color-blind*, refers to those agencies whose practices are not readily discernible. They

are "potentially" color-blind in that race is not referenced on their websites at all. There are a number of reasons (laid out in the text) to be suspect about whether such agencies are truly color-blind.

2. Other universal subject guides also draw upon the DMOZ for their directory results (e.g., Lycos and Netscape Search).

3. These estimates vary by category, agency, region, and year, with some estimating that staff costs range from 20 percent to 50 percent of agency operating costs.

4. What is typically not made explicit is that fees assessed adoptive parents for their desired child (e.g., white infant) may also defray the agency costs for other types of adoptions (e.g., special needs, minority, or adoption fees that are prorated).

5. In 2005, the adoption subsidy for private adoptions was raised to $10,390.

6. The names of programs are listed in the order of frequency found in both directories.

7. The separation of biracial from African American occurred with only a handful of agencies in the combined searches.

8. Since originally examining the website, these prices have been modified, with Latino placement fees now at $25,000 and African American fees remaining at $16,000.

9. For example, *Chicago Tribune*, December 28, 2003, "Parents Often Not Ready for Needy Foreign Kids," by Russell Working and Aamer Madhani: In this article, the writers outline issues of international adoption that are well documented in the literature of adoption and by some of the recent actions taken on the part of host countries. These issues include widespread issues of fetal alcohol syndrome, physical problems, developmental delays, and other problems associated with institutionalization (e.g., severe attachment disorders and post-traumatic stress).

10. These adoption professionals were persons with whom I became familiar both during my own adoption journey as well as through the process of tracking down information on adoption. None of these conversations were formal.

5

"Race Talk" in Adoption Forums

The Internet provides other indicators of the continued impact of race in adoption: adoptive parent profiles and forum discussions. Two major websites with adoptive parent profiles were examined at three time points between 2005 and 2006. Supplemented with information from other parent profiles, these websites illustrate racial demand and experiences of adoptive singles/couples using the Internet. Examination of archives from an online adoption forum and one advice column that encouraged interaction among adoptive families (www.nysccc.org) provides insights into how people view race and deal with racial matters.

ADOPTIVE PARENT PROFILES

Advertised as the "first Internet site [established in 1995] devoted to helping prospective adoptive parents and prospective birthparents meet," AdoptionOnline.com provides profiles of adoptive families to birth mothers. For a fee, the service offers two types of memberships to adoptive parents (Gold and Bronze levels) and allows birth mothers to select families along a number of dimensions: religion, lifestyle (suburban and urban), ethnic heritage, hobbies, occupations, and region. Another website, PotentialParents.com, advertises as a network of "loving families waiting to grow through open adoption." Families are presented according to type (single, couple, same-sex), location, religion, and "Other Children." A free service, Lifetimeadoption.com offers

adoptive families an opportunity to post letters to birth mothers, and birth
mothers can search adoptive families by region, keyword, or phrase, or peruse
an entire list of families. Though participation on these sites is relatively small
compared to the total number of adoption participants (from 80 or fewer
families on one site to over 300 on others), multiple searches (AdoptionNet-
work.com on November 13, 2005; April 20, 2006; and August 22, 2006, and on
ParentProfile.com on November 11, 2005; February 3, 2006; and August 28,
2006) enhance confidence in these sites as adequately reflecting the preferences of those who use the Internet to adopt.

Both websites presented here (AdoptionNetwork.com and ParentPro-
files.com) have memberships of over 200 adoptive couples and promote their
services in terms of the interactive nature of the Internet, transcendence of ge-
ographic limitations, and cost-effectiveness. Offering free consultation and
claiming an advertising budget of over $1 million annually, AdoptionNet-
work.com provides information to birth mothers and adoptive persons across
regions, religion, and ethnicity. ParentProfiles.com, perhaps the largest of the
adoptive parent networks, offers seven categories of information: state, region,
(child's) age, gender, ethnicity, special needs, and birth parents' religion.

The following table presents the racial/ethnic preferences of adoptive parents who used these networks. A total of seventeen racial/ethnic groups were
listed for AdoptionNetwork.com and nineteen groups for ParentProfiles.com;
however, only the nine comparable racial/ethnic categories between sites are
presented. These nine categories include African American, Asian, Caucasian,
Caucasian/African American, Caucasian/Hispanic, Caucasian/Asian, Hispanic, Multiracial, and Any Child. Categories that vary between websites, such
as Mediterranean, European, and Eastern European/Slavic/Russian are excluded since the number of adoptive parents choosing these categories was
negligible.[1]

Table 5.1 shows the relative size of each network, the total number of adoptive parents for all nine racial/ethnic categories, and the racial/ethnic demand
in domestic adoption. Supporting surveys of adoptive parents, these networks
show that white adoptive parents are the majority of network participants.
Similarly, relative demand for African American and biracial infants (African
American/Caucasian) is very small compared to other racial/ethnic groups.
Profiles also support the idea of a racial/ethnic hierarchy with greater demand
for Latino/Hispanic, Asian, and particularly mixed-ethnicity children (His-

Table 5.1. Racial/Ethnic Preferences of Adoptive Parents

	AdoptionNetwork.com			ParentProfile.com		
	(11/14/05)	(01/04/06)	(08/22/06)	(11/11/05)	(02/03/06)	(08/28/06)
African American	0	0	0	33 (4%)	25 (4%)	37 (5%)
Asian	12 (3%)	12 (3%)	8 (13%)	79 (9%)	63 (9%)	82 (11%)
Caucasian	171 (49%)	167 (48%)	126 (49%)	295 (35%)	255 (37%)	261 (34%)
Hispanic	28 (8%)	25 (7%)	14 (5%)	95 (11%)	77 (11%)	97 (13%)
African American/Caucasian	5 (1%)	3 (1%)	2 (1%)	49 (6%)	41 (6%)	60 (8%)
Hispanic/Caucasian	95 (26%)	91 (26%)	69 (27%)	197 (24%)	163 (24%)	182 (24%)
Asian/Caucasian	52 (14%)	52 (15%)	32 (12%)	81 (10%)	61 (9%)	31 (4%)
Multiracial	0	0	0	2	5	7
Any Child	2	0	4	4	0	3
Total	365	350	255	835	690	760

panic/Caucasian and Asian/Caucasian) by adoptive parents. These profiles are suggestive; however, discussions between adoptive parents (and occasionally birth mothers) offer insights into racial perspectives and adaptations of adoptive parents.

ADOPTION FORUMS

Adoption forums present online discussions or messages where participants reply to each other; however, unlike chat rooms, in which interaction is immediate, forums include responses that can occur significantly later than initial messages or postings. Some adoption forums maintain archives of the various topics covered. Archives from Adoption.com produced over 200 pages of conversations involving race. Searches were done on forums in Adoption.com, and like most Internet forums, a variety of threads (series of messages) were clustered under different topics. Discussions often generated new threads involving related issues.

Guidelines on Adoption.com's home page provided the parameters for interaction. As indicated in table 5.2, thread topics included transracial adoption; care of black and biracial children; and postadoptive experiences with children, family, school, and friends. Occasionally, a more general discussion of race (unrelated to adoption) occurred between forum participants. Ultimately, discussions were grouped in broader rubrics despite occasional overlap in subject discussions. For example, messages on hair and skin care elicited a response from one African American woman who raised questions about unexamined prejudice and white privilege. Because initial and dominant focus was hair and skin care, the conversation was categorized under this header. Though participants were largely adoptive parents, some birth mothers also posted responses. A number of participants identified as white, but there were also African American participants. Because self-identification was not consistent within or across threads, it was not possible to provide counts by race/ethnicity, gender, or role (e.g., birth parent). Several participants were active in these periods across threads, while others participated in only one thread. A few were regular participants (African American and white) who occasionally dominated one or more threads.

Verbatim posts and abbreviated conversations offered here typify responses to each topic, with spelling or punctuation modified to clarify comments. Participants are assigned anonymous initials in place of their online identifiers.

Table 5.2. Race Chat: Adoption Forums

Forum	Dates Searched	Archived Material	Thread Categories	Participants
Adoption.com		200+ pages	Family acceptance White privilege Rainbow families	Twenty-five parents Ten considering adoption Three birth mothers

	November 14, 2005–
	March 9, 2005
	June 16, 2006
			Racial identity
			Hair and skin
			Prejudice and racism
			Terminology
			African American
			  Placement and
			  "Supply"
			Color blindness
				Four transracial adoptees
				Three interested persons

NYSCCC.org		34+ pages	Unexpected prejudice Dilemmas of adopted	Six families Five considering adoption

	March 10, 2005–
	April 26, 2005
			Black children
			Discrimination in
			  transracial
			  adoption
			Race as primary
			  identity
			Transracial adoption
			  by gay families
				One birth mother
				Two transracial adoptees
				Three interested persons

Searches were conducted only on threads that indicated racial topics or when threads included racial issues in their headers (e.g., availability of black infants), but no formal comparisons were made between the total number of threads and those that focused on race. It is my guess (and one that could be examined) that the majority of threads on the Adoption.com forum paid little direct attention to race or racial matters and that threads on race primarily reflected the interests of either prospective or adoptive parents and adoptees involved in domestic transracial adoption. Adoptive parent profiles and the self-selection of forum participants are presumed to fit within the larger adoption picture where the relative demand for domestic transracial adoption, while perhaps growing, remains very small.

Ask the Experts, the New York State Citizen's Coalition for Children website (www.nysccc.org/answers), presented expertise of two transracial adoptees who responded to questions about race and adoption and encouraged posts from other readers. A search of this website was conducted from March 10, 2005 to April 26, 2005 and resulted in thirty-four pages of postings and included topics that overlapped with those in Adoption.com. Additional topics in Ask the Experts (not found in Adoption.com threads) are included here:

transracial adoption by white gay couples, perceived discrimination by white adoptive families, and "rainbow" families.

Aside from addressing the "demand" for black and biracial children and the implications about race evoked by these preferences, forum discussions present a zone of potential integration in cyberspace. What Mica Pollack (2004) called "race talk" or the cultural practices that involve "predictable scripts and silences" (11) is provided a space where we are able to address the question, What is the role of race in adoption? Adoption forums reveal attempts to reform racial meanings by promoting race talk and possibly interracial interactions. Posts suggest sensitive and seemingly well-intentioned efforts to understand and accommodate children with optimal care. However, several posts also generated debate among forum participants and between members of different races. Questions or comments from members of one group were frequently interpreted as naive, insensitive, misguided, or even racist by members of another group. Given the fact that the majority of participants who self-identified were white, it is perhaps not surprising that the topic of white privilege appeared throughout several threads. Peggy McIntosh (1989) likens white privilege to an invisible knapsack with "unearned assets that I can count on cashing in each day, but about which I was 'meant' to remain oblivious." Even though entitlement is typically unconscious when persons become involved in transracial adoption, issues involving white privilege inevitably emerge.

ADOPTION.COM

Race Chat: White Privilege

Prospective parents who asked for advice or information on transracial adoption often received responses that involved unacknowledged privilege. Some adoptive parents did not recognize white privilege, interpreting incidents as either normal or at least separate from race. Responding to another parent's experience of prejudice, one anecdote was met with several objections from both African American and white respondents:

P: It is interesting that you have found so many people who seem prejudice. Where we live, most people think our 2 boys, one Caucasian and one black American are cute together. My wife was at a children's museum once and a 3–4 year old child actually licked my black American son. Apparently he was told by someone that a child of color was made of chocolate; however, we have laughed over it. I am sorry to hear in your neck of the woods so many are still living in the past.

B: [in reponse to P] Curious children who mean no harm can cause much nonetheless. You can't protect your child from every experience where he is treated like an object, but you can reaffirm his humanity in the aftermath. Though I can understand that it's funny to you now, I am hoping that your wife's response to your child at the moment that incident occurred was different. I hope that she told him something to the effect that skin is skin, black or white, and told him how to respond the next time someone objectifies him. . . . Please don't take this as an attack as it is sincerely not my intent. My post is strictly in the spirit of this forum, raising healthy black children. . . . Of course my husband, to whom I spoke about this, thinks this is a fake story. As horrible as little kids were to me growing up, no one licked me, and I've frankly never heard of such a thing in all my years of blackness.

A number of experiences related to white privilege were described but not always seen as such. At the same time that "R" regards behavior and comments of strangers as supportive, and is irritated by inappropriate behavior, she or he fails to address such behaviors as explicitly linked to race and the unequal contexts within which children live.

R: I have only gotten positive responses from people [regarding R's African American son] and everywhere we go I swear we have 20 people coming up to tell us how cute he is. Although it could very likely be because our son IS the cutest child on the planet, I also think they are trying to show us that they support our decision to adopt transracially. It does, however, irritate me that we can't sit at a restaurant without people coming over and touching his hair, etc., without asking.

Like so many African American and biracial children who are subjected to inappropriate comments, questions, or crossing of physical boundaries, not everyone accepted privilege without questioning. For some, becoming the parent of a black or biracial child provided the catalyst for examining their position vis-à-vis their children. The mother of a biracial son acknowledged her epiphany regarding whiteness as the unmarked reference point from which others are judged:

> McK: At my children's day care, there is an AA [African American] man that brings his son (who is somewhere between 1 and 2 years old) around the same time I drop my kids off. His son is CC [Caucasian] and has red hair and green eyes. The situation makes me so curious. I am so disappointed in myself. I have many friends with multiethnic families and don't think twice about it, but when the situation is reversed from what is typical, I find myself as curious as those who question whether my son is mine or not. Sorry this is so long but I have just been so disappointed in myself about this situation. I was just disappointed that while I don't find anything unusual about a CC person or couple having AA kids, I do find it unusual for [an AA] person or couple to have a CC child.

Interestingly, and like the women in Ruth Frankenberg's hallmark study of whiteness (1993), what is "typical" is implicitly understood to be what is familiar, dominant—"white." Another parent offered advice to prospective adoptive families that incorporated recognizing color consciousness in America:

> S: Those of us who are white and raising children of color have to remember that our children will not benefit from our white privilege when we are not there. Yes, in a perfect world, all our children would be judged on the content of their character not the color of their skin. But sadly, that is not the case. My white boyfriends were never stopped for not looking like the neighborhood they were driving in. My black boyfriend was. When my white friends helped a friend move, police didn't ask what they were doing, but my black friend was stopped and questioned. My white friends didn't take special care to give cashiers their packages before they shopped or avoid putting their hands in their pockets so no one would accuse them of shoplifting, but my black friends had to do all those things and they did it almost without thinking, the way women don't list their first names in the phone book or have their keys in their hand long before they reach their car. And it wasn't a white guy who got shot 41 times because his wallet looked like a gun. Rather than shelter our children, we have to give them the tools to defend themselves. . . . It means talking about racism openly, whether it's a news story or a movie or something that happens on the playground. It means listening to our kids—and not denying that the world is the way it is.

Part of white privilege involves language and who gets to say what. Despite the argument of a postmodern society blurring racial/ethnic boundaries, race remains an important marker of identity. Processes of shifting power have been met with resistance by those who have traditionally maintained the right to name without reflection by consideration of those named. The significance of language is how it allows persons to consciously and unconsciously identify themselves through their linguistic choices. Adoption forums on race present particular opportunities in which persons can self-consciously engage in these discussions. Although the Internet is often regarded as highlighting language over such variables as race, gender, or class (Warschauer 2000), the discussion threads in these forums explicitly point to the interaction of race and language as persons debate, question, and investigate their newfound roles, experiences, and perspectives surrounding racial issues.

Race Categories: Taboo Words, or "Why Can't We Say That, Too?"

The common struggle over language involves not only "who gets to say what about whom" but also what doesn't get said. For example, one person asked why people of "mixed race" are frequently categorized as African American or black instead of biracial. A more provocative question involved the acceptable use of words by one group as opposed to another.

> R2: Some AA don't like "colored," some do; some don't like "black," some do; some don't like "brown," some do!! And why is it okay for AA to say something but not CC to say the same? I think it is ignorant to think that because CC children hear AA saying these things, which the AA child hears from his/her parents, and then CC children say it but get in trouble. I have seen it happen many times. If you want a word to stop being used, then I think EVERYONE should stop using it. I am not trying to be rude at all!! I am really interested and do not mean to be offensive:=)

As persons of color responded and challenged white privilege, the discussion in this thread became so heated that the forum moderator was required to remind participants of the rules for interaction.

> RA: I actually think it's quite ironic how some ethnic Caucasians get so upset that they are not allowed to use some word or phrase that another group finds offensive, yet that group can use it. How in the world is it any of your concern?

You know why it is wrong to use it if you are not a member of the group to whom it has historically referred and that the dominant group used it as a slur. Just don't use it. Period.

MML: What I want to know for those who are sooo against AA using the N-word, who are you to tell us we shouldn't take that word and use it in a positive light? Why does "white society" always have to take what we say and tell us what needs to be done and the right way to do it? It has been used negatively for many, many years, and now we use it amongst each other more positively or whatever means we want to use it and you want to take that from us. Also, why do you want to take what we say and use it in your vocabulary because you heard an AA say it and feel you should be able to say it? Why are you entitled?

MML's response resulted in a five-page dialogue with R2 at the end of which MML responded with the following.

MML: I really don't think blacks CARE what you or people with the same view as you think we should or should not use. No, YOU shouldn't use that word and I'm a little tired of those of your race telling me and others what we should or should not do, and I don't care that you don't listen to the music [referring to Rap music]. It is probably not meant for you. It's meant for those who can relate to the hardship of the lyrics in the music. I really don't care if you like the music or not. You really just prove my point on how "white society" still wants to have a grasp on how we live. Now who is racist?

The desire to transcend race sometimes took the form of refusing to acknowledge difference, thereby homogenizing the "other" and implicitly treating difference negatively. One participant rejected assigning her children to any racial categories, with the argument that racial difference (like any other difference) carries no evaluative character. This position also elicited several responses.

WD: My children are of mixed heritage. We do not talk about their skin color or why they are different from some people. We are all different and frankly I think it is great to teach my children that they are beautiful and that we all have our own uniqueness and love. I do not use descriptions like African American or white to describe others. As far as I am concerned, we are all UNIQUE and that's just how the world is supposed to be: diverse and wonderful. If someone says negative things about others because of their race, then I explain that I am perplexed by their lack of knowledge. Others can put people in categories if they so please, but I am raising my children that we are all members of one race, the human one.

J: The problem with that approach is that you are creating for your children a fantasy that is going to be shattered the minute they start school. Saying you don't see color or that it doesn't matter isn't true. It is our responsibility to teach our children the skills they need to cope and survive in a world that is majority [CC] driven. Our children pick up the subconscious messages in media, books, family and life. . . . I am fully aware that for a few short years my children will be known as the AA kids of a white mother and receive the privileges associated with that. But there will come a time (very soon, unfortunately) that they will have to know how to exist as men out in the world. They NEED me to prepare them for the different set of rules that exist out there because of the color of their skin. It would be fine and dandy for me to decide not to do that for them because that reality isn't fair, but then I would have failed them.

SP: The fact is, people DO put other people in categories and ignoring that is doing our children a disservice. Our children of color need to have the tools to deal with the racism and prejudice that they will face once they are away from us and our white privilege. While I share MLK's dream that one day our children will be judged by the content of their characters, not the color of their skin, I also am realistic enough to know that we're not there yet

As several scholars have pointed out, de-racing our language and maintaining adamantly color-blind positions may actually prevent us from shaping a new racial discourse that surpasses the limits of the present one and furthering equality among groups. Adoption forums present at least one public venue that allows and even encourages opportunities to create new patterns of interaction and new ways of speaking.

White privilege and race talk in forum discussions are inseparable, exemplifying how racial categories are created, contested, and sustained. Similar to the race talk found in school, discussions of race online provide yet another illustration of how matters involving race are simultaneously "color-mute and race-loaded" (Pollock 2004 74), and reflect the ongoing dilemma of when, how, and "who" should take race into account. Another topic of discussion involved availability of African American infants and biracial children. Interest in transracial adoption was delicately intertwined with family acceptance and race/color consciousness.

African American Supply and Placement

Inquiry into the need for adoptive parents of African American babies prompted responses about agencies soliciting transracial adoptions. Wait time for parents who adopted African American and biracial children varied between days and weeks, to over a year for placement. Adoptive parents perceived skin color to be an important part of the supply/demand issue.

> RD: In regards to L's note about skin color: DH [husband] and I have never cared what color our child's skin is, but when the agency was presenting pb-moms [prospective birth mothers] to us, they would say, "But they're very light-skinned" or "She's not that dark." Obviously, they were concerned that if the baby were "too black" we wouldn't want him/her. Before our home study was done, we were chosen by two different moms. The first was CC and the baby would be CC/AA. The second was totally CC. Then we were the second choice for an AA couple; they went with one of the two AA adoptive couples available through the agency. Now, we were chosen by an AA/CC pbmom (who is just AWESOME!). I thought that parents of AA babies wouldn't necessarily want to choose CC parents for them, but as the story shows, we were wrong.

> RC: One of the things to be aware of is that transracial families are very obvious and conspicuous. This means that you can rarely go anywhere or do anything without being stared at or asked probing questions by strangers. If you feel you can handle this sort of thing with grace and style, then welcome to the club.

Family Acceptance

Perhaps nowhere was race consciousness more meaningful to participants (particularly adoptive parents) than when it manifested in their nuclear and extended families. Only two people wrote about unexpected responses from partners; however, several comments noted rejection of adopted black and biracial children by grandparents, siblings, and in-laws that created anguish for adoptive parents.

> C: My DH and I have chosen our agency and seem to be on the track toward adopting an AA or biracial child. This will be our second adoption. We have a Hispanic daughter we adopted when she was a little over a year old. We are

happy and excited about our decision as are most of our friends and family—all except my mother. She is a widow in her mid 70s and is an even bigger bigot than Archie Bunker. I'm ashamed to even mention some of the comments she has made about African Americans. I've tried talking to her about her attitudes, confronting her, educating her, etc., and all I've wound up doing is making her defensive and hostile. She knows my husband and I are trying to adopt an AA or biracial child and she is not happy about it at all. She says she disagrees with our decision, has a right to her opinion, and won't be seen with me at Wal-Mart once we adopt our child, and on and on.

MK: The adoption of my son (a biracial child) will be finalized in 3 weeks. My aunt sent a card in which she congratulated my parents on their upcoming grandchild but that she still would be a grandparent first (her son and girlfriend are having a baby at the end of the year). This really hurt my feelings because my son is not even considered a grandchild. I have been upset ever since and have not spoken to my parents and even though they know I was hurt (through my sister), they have not attempted to explain or apologize. With the holidays coming up, it is just going to be hard not to have family involved. Now I am wondering what harm I am doing to my son.

K12: I can't offer any advice, but I can tell you that you aren't alone. My daughter (not finalized yet) is biracial. She is accepted by the majority of the family, but in some ways, I feel this is only because her birth mother is Caucasian. I only have major issues with one family member—my grandfather, who ironically is my mother's adopted father! He doesn't want anything to do with my daughter and simply tolerates her presence when they are in the same house once a year. . . . Do not subject your son to prejudiced people within the family—he will find enough of that outside your family within our society that fears anyone different from themselves. Also, children sense the unspoken prejudice, fear, etc., and they see the sideways glances and sense the tension between you and the relative in question. Always remember the most important relationship your son has is with YOU, not your mother or siblings or anyone else. If you have a healthy relationship with him, that is the only thing that really matters.

Rejection by family was not limited to African American and biracial or even adopted children, but also included Asian and Hispanic children. Some parents responded by severing all ties with family members, while others struggled to gain acceptance.

CH: My husband is Asian. I never sensed any bad feelings about it while we were dating or getting married. [It] came as quite a shock when my fundamentalist Christian mom suggested I consider having an abortion when we excitedly announced we were expecting a baby a few months after our wedding. Eight years and 2 children later her face still freezes when someone comments on how her granddaughter looks like a little Japanese doll. And while she adores my daughters from my first marriage (to a Caucasian), my two younger kids are clearly an embarrassment. I would have married my husband in spite of her views and it wouldn't have stopped our decision to have children together, even if I had seen it coming, but if I had a choice of choosing whether to accept a placement of a child from an ethnicity that would undoubtedly cause a rupture in the family, I think I'd have to give it a lot of thought, not to reward someone's prejudice, but because I'd want my child to have the most supportive family environment possible. . . . My mother's reaction has led us to drastically change our relationship with her in order to protect the feelings of our younger children, who are now old enough to understand what is going on, and this has meant strain between me and my mother and some loss of contact between my older girls and their grandmother. It's unfortunate and very painful at times for me as her daughter to see her in that light but it's not something I can do much about. The kids come first. One thing I have learned is that while we can change ourselves, we cannot change others, particularly if they don't think they need/want to change.

Some parents offered positive stories of initial family rejection that turned around.

TP: Our son is AA and we are CA [Caucasian]. I am from the most racist family. My grandparents were so against being friends with, talking to, and interacting with blacks, and so on, and although my mom and dad weren't necessarily "racist," they raised us daughters to only date white, so until a year and a half ago when I brought my son home I NEVER would have looked twice at an AA man for a relationship just because I had been raised that way. When DH and I began searching for a child, I felt we could only look for biracial and CC babies or children because I could maybe "hide" it better than if they had AA in them. OMG [Oh my God]! After a few months of thinking and praying DH and I really started relooking at ourselves and skin color. We got the call about our son THREE times before we said yes, mostly out of fear for us crossing that silent family barrier. After the third call, we KNEW God was telling us this was our child and booked our flight and picked up our son totally blindfolded! Heck, I not only had NO clue about anything AA-related, also I had a very irate family waiting for me when we would arrive home with our blessing. Our son came to us physically not taken care of, as well as very delayed due to the bio[logical] family neglect, so we sure did have LOTs to learn in a 24-hour time frame! At first my family made me so angry, and then they made me sad. How could they refuse this beautiful baby due to his skin? Grandpa would say on the phone nasty comments that I will spare from my post, and my mom was upset that I was upsetting everyone like this. How could I do this to them?! Well, here I sit typing, almost laughing at them now a year and a half later. It took a few months and lots of stress BUT you would never guess who is our son's favorite now ... you guessed it, my grandma and grandpa! They love him to pieces and he is SO bonded to them, it's amazing. My mom lost her attitude a lot quicker as she has younger children still at home of her own and their honest purity for the race issue made her realize he was a child not a color to judge. Today you would never think he was black when he is with her ... she loves him as much, too, and she is his "mamaw." It's hard to pull him away from her sometimes!

Whether "whitewashing" her son's color was unconscious, a misspoken statement or an indicator of personal predispositions ("Today you would never think he was black"), this mother's intention was clearly to show family acceptance of her son and that people can change. And while "change" grounded in tokenism, whitewashing, or color-muting may well be offensive to many, particularly persons of color, these participants appeared sincere in wanting to show that change is possible. Several white parents commented on positive responses their children received from others, even strangers. Like many adoptive families, parents of African American and biracial children were sometimes told how "noble" they were for saving their children. These same sentiments, however, were not always available when the situation was reversed. As mentioned in the last chapter, the concept of minority or transracial adoption in America is not a new phenomenon regardless of how it is now portrayed. Though white interest in transracial adoption has historically been very limited, African Americans have long been willing to adopt (both formally and informally) biracial children. Brought to our attention by such early twentieth-century stories as the Great Arizona Orphan Abduction (Gordon 1999) when Irish orphans adopted by Mexican parents were kidnapped by angry white vigilantes, tolerance found for transracial adoption continues to depend upon the assumptions of which groups will do the adopting (saving?) and which groups will be adopted (saved).

K: What do you think about the situation being reversed? Let's say a black couple adopts a white child and raises them in a community that is 95 percent black. I have a friend who fosters in a predominantly black community, and she and her husband are also both AA. They recently had two teenage foster sons who were white and she laughed as she told me about some of her experiences. But some of their experiences weren't very funny. There were several people who felt that it was just fine for white couples to adopt AA children, but felt there was something wrong with these white children being in an AA foster home.

Color Consciousness

For many participants, awareness of color consciousness emerged after adopting children of color and as their children aged.

D: Our son was born AA/CC/AI [African American/Caucasian/American Indian] and he was amazing. I was unsure about adoption, but the biracial card made it all that much harder since we didn't know 'til he was born. We have moved to a great neighborhood and school district, but he is definitely a minority and I refuse to move to a more diverse area. My son's skin color should not decide where we live! I protect him from the remarks but my car was set on fire, I was called a slave owner and an N-lover, etc. My husband is 14 years my senior and has had few remarks, but they only attack a female here. I won't ignore them. I confront them and make it clear that I will not tolerate this in any way (without my son present of course). I feel angry all the time.

E: My husband and I just finalized on the adoption of our two precious daughters who happen to be African American. We also live in a very Southern state where there is a lot of racism. We knew when we decided to adopt these girls that there would be a lot of people who didn't agree with what we were doing. We didn't care! We have several friends and co-workers who are AA and they have been totally supportive. We have encountered AAs in public places (total strangers) and none have ever made me or my children feel that we didn't belong together. As a matter of fact, I have had so many offers of help from AA ladies that I can pick and choose who to call if I have a question. We have, however, encountered numerous rude remarks and stares from the CC people we've come in contact with. There are many CC people that we know who do not think that we should have adopted outside our race, and they haven't hesitated to let us know. And believe me, I didn't hesitate in letting them know where the door was, if you know what I mean. In my experience, the white people are the majority of the people who have a problem with it. Maybe it's just where we live, like I said—it's the Deep South. You would think the Civil War was still going on!

Such descriptions ultimately resulted in a lengthy response from MML, a regular participant who never hesitated to offer a different perspective on a number of issues, including the subjects of rescue and ignoring the prejudiced responses of neighbors.

MML: I had to voice on the things that were being said on some of the postings and say how offended I was. I'm told to give people a break because they are taking in kids. . . . There were some things said on this board that were really ignorant. This is what I'm trying to say, you have to understand what things can be insulting and offensive to people of different races and . . . that some things you say being white to someone black can be an issue.

MML: [in response to "why give a hoot what our neighbors think?"] If you live in a neighborhood where a child is not welcome, you best believe that child is going to live in a hell that you won't be able to imagine. People are so cruel and ignorant especially of difference. And don't let this child be one of those that doesn't want to bring the problems home and deal with it . . . it's not that different when a child is in a school [where] many don't like [him or her] and that child is constantly teased and beat up on. Many parents place their kids (the ones being bullied) in a different school setting and the child is happier. Shouldn't that be your goal as well and not [to] prove that those in your neighborhood can like it or not? That's being so defensive like you or whoever is trying to prove a point. . . . This child already knows he/she is different and then there are others that put it out there in an even more negative and nasty way. . . . What point are you trying to make? What does living in a prejudiced neighborhood have to do with raising your kids to be proud of whom they are and not live their lives as victims? The child can do that in a neighborhood where he/she feels safe.

SM: I'm a single mom of an adopted black child, and up until this point have either been deaf and dumb to the racial comments or there just haven't been any until now. My daughter's 4 and getting more and more active with children and their families, and I can't keep from getting angry when ignorant people make ignorant comments yet this is happening more and more with so-called friends, family, and co-workers. I know I can't fight the whole world, even though right now it feels like her and I against it. I just want someone else's ideas on how I can work through this. . . . There is nothing more painful than to take your child to the park and watch families silently collect their children or run them over to other park items all because a minority and a mixed child (adopted or not) wants to play. . . . My beautiful lite brown child with blond hair has been noticing just how different people are and even asks why. The really sad thing is that if she goes to the slide to have fun and other kids are around, they are mean to her.

RB: I was working in a town about 40 miles away. I managed the store so I took her [biracial daughter] with me often, and a customer who was white asked me if my baby's mother laid in a tanning bed while she was pregnant, as she knew she was adopted. . . . Most white people don't say much to us but they notice. . . . Since she has been in the first grade, my little girl says she has a boyfriend who has blond hair and blue eyes. Another little girl in class told her that she couldn't marry him because she was brown and he was white. Then we were really hit with the issue recently with our failed adoption of her siblings on another thread. I mean that really hit home how much race is such an issue with some people.

One preschooler's experience highlighted the lack of intentionality or awareness where color was concerned. Her mother noted the teacher's color chart for behavior: green = good, yellow = warning, red = note home, black = parents called.

M: I asked the teacher . . . why are you using black? My child's father is black—do you not see how this can be used subliminally to affect my child's self-esteem and how it can teach nonblack children to equate black with bad? She had never considered it, had borrowed it from another teacher. . . . Also, that year my beautiful daughter came home telling me she wished she had blond hair and blue eyes and white skin.

MP: I am finding that my sweet 10-year-old Peruvian daughter (who has more the appearance of a biracial child) is very sad and moody of late. I was not ready for this personality change, but looking back I can remember numerous times when she was forced into the role of outsider in play groups. At this age, with adolescence coming on very quickly, she is much more volatile about it all and I, too, have found our church to be lacking in resources (or interest) in helping with such problems. My daughter is just kind of lost there. . . . When they [church members] call, I am hoping it is to inquire as to how we are, but it is usually just to ask for more of my time volunteering, etc. The racial issue is one most white people wish would just go away. No one wants to hear about it.

Hair and Skin

Two threads focused on skin and hair care of African American and biracial adoptees. Again, race talk involving adjectives like "nappy" was constructed and contested by those adopting children of color and by African Americans.

MML: It is so different, and I don't know the best way to explain this. [I'm] not saying everyone or whichever race would look at this the same, but understand that many do and that the child in your care just may be that one. You know the child sees the difference and children love to be the same as their parents, adopted or whatever. When you are stating the obvious difference [nappy] without any malice or anything, that child [already] knows [that difference]—the continuous lotioning of the skin or that special lotion that he/she needs and the small amount you have. The difficulty of having their hair done and the ease of doing yours or any other child with a "better" strand of hair. We all know how small kids are and they pick up things easily. AA use these terms from generation to generation as well as their own hair to this day. Everyone wants to say that we are all the same but it's different for many. This is where knowing AA heritage and you would understand that in past generations whites made it to be ugly. I do understand that you do not mean anything from it because you hear it coming from an AA person and may think its fine to describe a child's hair and skin the same way.

R: I just think that if you ignore what many people on this board say by just saying that they don't know better, then that's what they are going to keep on doing and let their ignorance be their excuse for not knowing. It's no different when ignoring what a child does because they don't know better and that child will keep on doing it until they are finally corrected. They need to know that a black person's skin isn't ashy—it's dry skin and may just need lotion, or they may have eczema. I saw on one board where a woman used "nappy" to describe her child's hair. How does this person speak around the child when doing this child's hair? . . . One woman on this board had an AA child when she was an infant and when [the girl] hits 2 1/2 years old, now she's wondering if she made the right choice. Are you kidding me?!

Rainbow Families

It was not uncommon for families to have both biological and adopted children, and nearly half of the posts on this topic described different experiences for adopted children, particularly when they were black or biracial. One parent described how people responded differently to her biracial child than to her blond and blue-eyed biological child. Some adoptive families were "rainbow" families with children from different racial/ethnic backgrounds (e.g., Asian, African American, and/or Hispanic). A parent of six multiethnic children said she and her husband frequently discussed color consciousness.

L: It is ALL (not shouting; emphasis only) about the skin tone . . . how dark it is, nothing else. It doesn't seem to matter who is talking about it. This is the same reason some couples cannot adopt a darker pigment African American child but they can adopt a Caucasian/African American child. It's the reason some people can easily accept the Asian child, because they have lighter SKIN TONE and are not as dark as many African American children. Crazy, isn't it?! And we have met caseworkers who feel the very same way. I was once told by an agency (out of country, years ago) that I was TOO pale to adopt a biracial child (Japanese/African American) but my husband (who is darker complexion) would have been all right! I know, I can hardly believe it, do you? But it's true! . . . And we humans are supposed to be "higher thinking" hmmmmmm.

After reading a number of posts on how families help their adoptive children to attain a sense of self, an African American (and regular participant) spoke out.

JL: I sat and read the posting for "helping children be proud of their brown skin." All I can say is UNBELIEVEABLE!! I'm just blown away that those of you that have foster/adopted kids are quick to pick up a book. How many of you have friends that are African American and other races [that are the same] as your kids? And one just don't cut it. How many times have you had other races at your home for dinner? . . . I'm an African American woman. I have friends of many races. Instead of reading a book and trying to follow instructions you need to talk one on one with those who are the race of the kids in your home. . . . Instead of saying your skin is beautiful, tell that child he/she is beautiful. Children ask all types of questions. . . . It's obvious to me those that posted on that board are not friends of those of different races—especially of their foster/adopted kids—because you wouldn't need a book. Knowing those from your job does not count, unless they came to dinner more than 2 times at your house. I applaud that you guys took these kids in but can do nothing but shake my head at what I read. The sad thing about it is that you guys have NO CLUE that anything you posted is so insulting for someone of my race.

Recent studies on cyberspace estimate that persons of color comprise only 2 percent of Internet users (Leon 2007) and African American participants on these threads often expressed feeling "overwhelmed" by other participants. It was not uncommon to have an ongoing dialogue among thread participants (presumably CC participants, though not all identified as such) evoke a response from an African American that also served as catalyst for comments from other AA participants. JL's response is one example.

JB: When I read this post I thought, I'm the only African American on this board and people don't realize the things that come out of their mouths. I read one post where a woman "WW" states that she grew up around AA and knows about ashyness and hair. How ignorant is that? And she's thinking about adopting a black child. Your heart may be good but the fact that the things that are said by some on this board are mind-boggling. How are you going to have different race in your home and not realize the ignorance that comes out of your mouth!!

A few adoptive parents pointed out how their racial identity changed as they began parenting a black or biracial child.

J: I know for CERTAIN that my racial identity is now different. I am no longer the white mama of a black child. I am a part of a multiracial family and that IS my identity—it also allows me acceptance and access to a minority world which I could never have understood prior to parenting black sons. I also know my Caucasian children see race very differently than their peers. Anyway, just a suggestion.

Color Blindness

To what extent did forum participants regard our society as color-blind? Several adoptive parents described generally positive experiences and characterized their social mileu as one of acceptance and support. Other parents indicated changes in perceptions of society as their children grew older and entered school or other social activities. Thus, the idea that racial identification and awareness changes for adoptees (the focus of scholars like Richard Lee [2003]) may also be applied to adoptive parents. Descriptions of positive experiences were also laced with comments and behaviors that some might interpret differently than did these parents. Perhaps it should not be surprising to find racial optimists among persons actively engaged in crossing racial borders and it is fair to suggest that the majority of adoptive parents cautiously viewed color blindness as an emerging reality.

In some cases, color blindness was solidly part of a parent's belief system and she or he appeared determined to maintain it.

E: We adopted 4 AA children four years ago and we are both CC. We live in a predominantly white area where my children are four of only a few AA children at school. We do go to an AA church, which was deliberate on our part so the kids would have friends and role models that were AA. However, my kids are thriving and it doesn't seem to faze them that mom and dad are white. WE are raising them the same way we raised our birth children. I see no difference in raising black vs. white children, except that you must build a sense of pride in them of their history. Of course, what's funny to me is that when they came to me (ages 5, 7, 9, 11), they didn't know anything about their AA heritage even though they had been in AA homes, so I'm not sure of what the issue of CC parents raising AA children (or any other race) is. You really do need to be aware of the prejudices that your children must face, which I admit I was blind to as a white person. You learn that fast, though. Best of luck with whatever race your children are and if you love them, the rest works itself out.

P: I have received wonderful support and an amazing sense of community since adopting my daughters. I have gotten a few unkind stares, but they have been few and far between. Mostly I get comments on how beautiful the children are, what wonderful people me and my husband must be to have "saved" these children, to which I always reply that we didn't adopt to be wonderful people, we just wanted babies, and it was the children who saved us.

ST: The white community trips over themselves sometimes trying to shower approval on us. I know that deep down maybe they have some issues with race that they haven't resolved, but our experience has been only positive. Our family and friends have been as happy for us as they could be. It has been wonderful and no one cares that he looks different. They respect that he is AA but they love him as much as my BIO [biological] son. Unfortunately, and much to my surprise, all the negatives we have encountered have been by people who are AA. My only concern is now that our son won't ever be accepted by the black community because we are white.

A: Forgive me if I offend anyone with this next statement, but there is FAR too much emphasis placed on racial differences. I do not buy into the theory that there are cultural differences between races based solely on their color of skin, shape of their eyes, or texture of their hair. I, of Scot/English/German descent, am no less or no more white than my Yemeni or Polish neighbors, yet I don't have the same culturally based practices as they do. . . . Believe me, I am well aware that my son is biracial and I don't need anyone to point that out or remind me of it, but that is NOT the reason I love my son. . . . A child should not be raised to identify him/herself as anything other than who they are, individually and as a member of family. Race and skin color are matters of genetics, just as blue eyes and brown hair are. It is not a matter of situation and condition in life. When we all STOP PLAYING the "CARD" and BLAMING THE OTHER RACE FOR OUR OWN SELF-DESTRUCTIVE BEHAVIORS the world will be a much better place.

Whether through good intention, white privilege, lack of racialized experiences, or a sense of benign indifference to the ignorance of others, some parents maintained a stubborn denial of racial difference even as their experiences pointed to it (e.g., occasional stares, licking of a child, setting fire to a car). It is also important to remember that the picture of family life (adjustments, problems, or lack thereof) is painted by parents, not adoptees, and it is difficult to infer the cognitive, emotional, and long-term consequences of racialized experiences for children (an issue that continues to be debated in adoption circles). The belief of a few participants was that they now lived in a color-blind world with others determined to fashion one. Still others struggled and questioned how best to live in what they regarded as a racially ordered world. For all of these persons, forum discussions demonstrate how race continued to play a part in their everyday lives and talk, particularly those who dared to cross racial boundaries.

NYSCCC.ORG

The advice column *Ask the Experts* is a forum where participants shared stories, offered advice, or discussed ways in which race matters. Beliefs presented here often overlapped with those presented in the Adoption.com forums, but some topics were unique to this forum.

Are We Prejudiced?

Though many discussions in Adoption.com revolved around availability of black and biracial children and the challenges of raising children from a different cultural background, no direct statements or questions were asked about the appropriateness of transracial adoption or possible biases of adoptive parents. Indeed, one explanation for the small percentage of domestic transracial adoptions (Roberts [2002] estimates this as 1–4 percent) is that white couples feel inadequate to properly parent black children. In this forum a participant reflected on his thoughts about transracial adoption and questioned his values, inviting others to respond.

> JP: Our reasons for wanting to adopt in our own race are that first, we would like our baby to look like us; second, that although we have friends of other races and could seek out and make new friends in our child's race, this may be contrived; and third, we truly believe that a child is best raised within his/her own race. . . . Do you think our desire to adopt within our own race is an indication of prejudice, ignorance, or shortsightedness, or do you think this is how most of the world would react?

Race was not the only consideration in transracial adoption as sexual orientation added yet another dimension to the discussion.

Transracial Adoption by White Gay Couples

> WG: We are a white male couple and live in Los Angeles but in a pretty white neighborhood. We have many gay friends who have created families through adoption. We also don't have any friends of color, not by choice, it's just how it turned out. We are very open to the idea of a transracial adoption, but we are

concerned that the combination of having two dads layered on top of racial identity issues would be a lot to ask of a child.

AL: As a white gay male I admit that I am also conservative. Even so, I have been thinking about adopting an African American or biracial child. I believe my partner and I could do a decent job, but I (we) am wondering whether it would make more sense to adopt a Hispanic or Asian child. My (our) perception is that it would be more difficult to raise a black child in a white home. Any and all advice is welcome.

JR: Only you know your prejudices about race and how you feel about parenting black, Hispanic, or Asian children. As I mentioned to another couple with these considerations, the racism visited upon African Americans has resulted in the fact that black-white relations are fraught with difficulty. The consequence is that adoption of black children by white parents is problematic because such adoptions take place in a larger sociopolitical context.

Here participants are not engaging in race talk so much as self-conscious interrogation of motives regarding race.

Reverse Discrimination?

Both white and black families perceived discrimination by adoption agencies. Interestingly, more posts claiming discrimination were made by blacks who maintained that adoptive access to children of their own race as well as to white children is prohibited in favor of white adoptive families. For example, one African American argued in the following way.

V: Why is it that black children are quick to be placed with white families but the same doesn't seem to happen when the children are white? I'm a black mother of two and my son's friend (11 y.o. [years old]) with whom he played with daily and his 5 y.o. brother have been in the system for over 3 years, and when it came to my attention that they were up for adoption, I went through and passed all the necessary steps. BUT after I made my desire for them known, I was sternly discouraged and told not to pursue them due to the fact their family was very racist and they had a bad experience with a black foster family in the past. Needless to say, on my drive home I was in tears. My family's situation and existing bonds to the boys were never considered. Also, the boys were never asked or presented with us as a potential family. . . . It's obvious that MEPA [Multi-Ethnic Placement Act] didn't apply to me, and why is it I wasn't good enough to adopt them boys but since then have been presented with two other black children?

V: I was recently passed over for a white couple in adopting three siblings ages 2–6, and I am an educated professional woman. I know that if I applied for a white, blond-haired, blue-eyed baby, my chances would be slim and none. Nonetheless I have to compete with white yuppies for the new young black children who are available for adoption.

D: I don't know your situation, but couldn't it be that they thought a couple would be better for 3 children than a single? . . . I'm also wondering why there are so many black children available for adoption?

V: Maybe they did feel so, but that doesn't make it so. Younger children are few, and most white couples prefer them over older children. The younger kids have less baggage, and black families now have to compete for them with more affluent white couples. In this case, they were going to split up a trio of sisters until I inquired about all three, which seemed to up the ante for the white couple. There are a lot of politics involved in the adoption industry. . . . The fact that economic affluence isn't the most important factor in parenting these children does not seem to matter. I still believe that a mature, educated black woman would be a better choice for a young or black infant child, and so does the Association of Black Social Workers, by the way. As a black woman, I am far more experienced in raising black children than any white woman, single or married . . . the law [MEPA] is being used to excuse workers from attempting to recruit black families. . . . I've talked to adoption facilitators who say they have to fight to get the social workers to consider black families they have waiting, so I'm not some crazy conspiracy theorist.

Participants were generally sympathetic and responded with encouragement to pursue the adoptions either through the adoption agencies or other means, such as the American Civil Liberties Union. However, as is often the case when race (and racism) are identified by persons of color, alternative answers were offered redirecting attention to placement away from being a racial issue. "V"s defensive response denying she was a "conspiracy theorist" signals what

McIntosh (1989) cites as a daily effect of white privilege: "If I declare there is a racial issue at hand, or there isn't a racial issue at hand, my race will lend me more credibility for either position than a person of color will have."

Race as Primary Identity

Despite our postmodern world and theories of identities as multiple, dynamic, and conflictual, several African Americans regarded race as *the* primary identity of a person, shaping and limiting a person's life. This view was often not shared by whites.

> PP: I would like to know whether for an African American child growing up in a white family—even if surrounded by other African American people—race would become THE issue, THE main source of identity? As an immigrant, I have experienced a certain amount of prejudice in America and often have been told about my country of origin rather than asked. I have a background in cross-cultural studies and a cross-cultural marriage. I know how important race, culture, nationality are for one's identity. At the same time, I have learned that there are deeper sources of identity (relationship with God/universe, belonging to humankind) that have to support the other elements. When I came to this country, due to the fact that my country was viewed in a stereotyped way, I tended to over assert my nationality, make it the main source of my identity. I wonder if this could also happen to a black child growing up in a white family, that he would make his race the main and only source of identity.

One of the most hopeful threads was a question asked (and answered) by JN about fundamental changes brought about through her participation in transracial adoption: "Before you adopted, did any of you contemplate how adopting transracially would change YOUR racial identity?"

> JN: Somewhere your choices stop being for your children and who they are and are just because it's who your family is and who you are. We are a black family just as much as we are a white family. Thirty years from now when I'm a grandmother in a room surrounded by my children, their spouses, and my grandchildren, I will probably be the only Caucasian in the room. Through the process of this adoption I have challenged how I personally, racially, culturally identify in a way that I never thought about before I began this journey.

CONCLUSION

Profiles of adoptive parents and postings from forum archives provide another view into the role of race in adoption. Much like Pollock's schools, our racialized order on the Internet, and more importantly in private adoption, occur through commercialization (advertising and commodifying), delineation and separation of racial bodies, thereby regulating and rewarding according to different race-based adoption programs. Analogous to the process occurring in schools, private adoption incorporates different discourses surrounding children and false assumptions about children, particularly black and biracial children. Because of the anonymity of cyberspace the Internet has been called a deracialized environment where race can be as prominent or nonexistent as one wants it to be. Discussions in Internet forums and chat rooms present us with opportunities to take on the challenge of confronting and rebuilding the type of society that so many argue is already here. Regardless of efforts to cross the racial divide, and despite the potential of the digital divide, beliefs, events, and experiences of most transracial families, birth parents, and adoptees posting on these forums continue to be inextricably tied to race, or as Pollock (2004, 13–14) surmises, "We don't belong to simple race groups, but we do," and "Race doesn't matter, but it does."

NOTE

1. Parents were given three opportunities to list their racial/ethnic preferences on the network membership form. In these searches, approximately 80 percent provided only one preference in ParentProfile.com and 92 percent in AdoptionNetwork.com. Other parents listed up to three preferences, presumably rank ordered; however, it is not possible to determine whether all preferences were tabulated for each adoptive parent/couple or whether the summaries offered reflect only the first preference of parents. This analysis includes only the first preference listed.

Transnational, Transracial, and Minority Adoption and Public Policy

America's current racial/ethnic diversity is the greatest in its history. We have seen new challenges to the existing social order: no longer do racial/ethnic and immigrant groups adopt a posture of assimilation. Instead, new demands are made on America. Immigration marches in March, May, and July of 2006 showed the burgeoning power of immigrant groups as they protested criminalization of undocumented workers and influenced immigration reform. We have also witnessed a backlash against these demands with the rise of nationalism, xenophobia, and color-blind racism. Color-blind ideology has privatized the discourse on social issues and neoliberal policies have exacerbated inequalities, discouraging support for public education in favor of school choice, dismantling social welfare programs in favor of workfare, and undermining preservation of the ecology in favor of corporate entrepreneurship. Institutional and interpersonal relations are now refracted through the lens of extreme individualism, and adoption is no exception.

Changing discourses and definitions of race in America are reflected in private domestic adoption. Despite these changes, race remains a salient factor in who gets adopted. Websites of private agencies reveal that color consciousness continues to pervade our society. These sites also show how racial categories are shifting, as not all persons of color are located similarly. The tripartite system of racial categories described by Eduardo Bonilla-Silva (2001) finds its analogy in private adoption, with several websites separating children into three categories and showing how the term *biracial* is used almost exclusively for children of any ethnic group mixed with African American heritage. At the same time, other children, particularly those who are mixed with white ethnic parents, are given honorary white status, removed from minority and biracial programs, and placed into a middle category between the traditional and biracial/minority programs or into the traditional or "Caucasian" program. Private adoption websites illustrate a world largely circumscribed by racial categories along with the power of race for distributing privilege in interpersonal and institutional exchanges. As privatization has increasingly dominated our world and disparities between and within countries has grown, globalization, racism, and adoption intersect and generate new meaning for human rights. Issues are no longer national—they are global.

INTERCOUNTRY ADOPTION

In 2005, the U.S. State Department reported that intercountry adoptions by Americans had more than doubled in the past decade, matched by an increase in private agencies facilitating these adoptions.[1] Because many of these agencies also maintain domestic and minority adoption programs, private domestic and intercountry adoption are not completely separate practices. Agencies that facilitate both types of adoption are basically self-policing, and the amount of money expended on domestic and intercountry adoption is often comparable for adoptive parents.

Currently, twenty-six states recognize adoptions processed in other countries; seventeen states require re-adoption (via petition); and eighteen states have no provisions for intercountry adoptions (NAIC 2003). Though regulations have been drawn up by the U.S. State Department, projected ratification of the Hague Convention treaty is some time in the next two years. Some fear that the proposed U.S. framework for implementing the Hague treaty fails to secure the rights and welfare of adoptees and their families. Complicating the issue is the contribution of adoption to the political economies of nations, with estimates of annual income ranging from $200 million to $400 million. Such contributions are clearly more significant for sending countries than for receiving ones. However, Kim Park Nelson (cited in Trenka 2005) estimates that when ancillary adoption businesses are included (clothing, dolls, magazines, books), adoption becomes a billion-dollar industry for the United States.

Emphasis by some U.S. scholars, social workers, and adopters has been on the lack of a legal framework to facilitate intercountry adoption and the necessity of streamlining the process for adoptive parents rather than protecting the rights of families in sending countries. A survey of 1,600 intercountry adoptive families signaled a number of problems with the system: (1) nearly 75 percent of families had been asked to carry cash ($3,000 or more) to pay for additional fees; (2) 14 percent indicated their agency had withheld, or provided inaccurate, information about the adoption process; (3) 14 percent reported they would not recommend their agencies to others. Figures for dissatisfaction were even higher for those families working with agencies to adopt children from Russia (Freidmutter 2002). The focus on the rights and dilemmas of adoptive parents by scholars and politicians has often led to claims of exaggeration of child laundering. Instead of a global and highly interconnected picture of the impact of postindustrial countries on developing ones, Americans often get a picture of the internal failures of nations to secure their children's futures.

Law professor David M. Smolin explains how difficult it is to obtain evidence of corruption in the adoption process due to the nature of the activity.

> Those who traffic, buy or steal children for processing through the adoption system do not advertise their illicit activities. Moreover, most within the adoption system, including adoption agencies, adoptive parents, and sometimes even adoptees, have motivations for minimizing or ignoring evidence of such conduct. . . . Logically, the vast majority of such cases would never come into public view, for the illicit aspects of the case would remain hidden under the legitimating veil of legal adoption. These abuses of the adoption system could not last long if they were not usually hidden; these crimes would not exist if they were not usually successful in achieving the aims of their perpetrators. (2005, 1–3)

Smolin (2005) cites a variety of inducements used to get families to part with children, such as being told they will be able to stay in touch with their children or that they will receive continuing financial support from adoptive parents. Though several countries have good reputations in intercountry adoption (China, Ukraine, and Russia), there are also several with bad reputations, such as Cambodia, Guatemala, India, and Vietnam. In the past fifteen years, seventeen of forty sending countries to the United States placed either a temporary or permanent moratorium on private adoption because of suspected or known abuses of children and families (though not necessarily by U.S. citizens or private agencies). UNICEF (United Nations Children's Fund; n.d.) also cautions against poor control of intercountry adoption and cites this activity as one cause of the child trade.

One of the most important criticisms of adoption literature is the bias of "who gets to talk." Critics maintain that construction and presentation of adoption reflects the social location of adoption participants. Whereas scholars and intercountry adopters are often given a forum for their views to influence public policy, literary activist Jane Jeong Trenka (2005) observed, "Adoptees are viewed as perpetual children, with views easily dismissed as 'angry,' 'ungrateful,' or 'bitter,' especially if our views are politicized, raced, or consider the women who gave birth to us." An assumption by adoption advocates that children are better off than with their birth parents is often coupled with the argument that if poorer nations were truly concerned with the needs of children, they would support international adoption. Trenka has countered that if individual and national advocates of intercountry adoption were truly concerned with the status of poor children, they would work on ways to secure the maintenance of families in these countries rather than taking their children. "The pattern that emerges is a collective cultural trauma on a global scale, manifested through the bodies of children and the mothers they have been taken from. It is an accepted, admired, praised, seemingly benevolent programme of forced assimilation and amnesia, of relatively rich women entitling themselves to the children of severely impoverished and desperate women. It is a program of complicity in the so-called sending countries and unbridled greed for the natural resource of children in receiving countries. It is a program of ignorance enforced by the adoption industry itself" (Trenka 2005).

Another argument suggests constructions of different groups of children help shape the adoption market in ways that promote transnational adoption over domestic adoption.

"This makes their children (of intercountry adoption) the innocent of the innocent—a bare canvas upon which American-ness can be reproduced, an image not just of (adoptive) parents, but of the supremely modern. In the case of children from the former socialist bloc, the narrative of rescue adds an appealing layer of heroism: not only are these children innocent of the political choices of the former leaders of their nations, but their successful upbringing also confirms the U.S. victory in the Cold War" (Ortiz and Briggs 2003, 42).

The narrative of white families turning from domestic to transnational adoption fails to establish the nexus between processes of racialization and the specific countries to which Americans turn. Eighty-five percent of transracial adoptions by U.S. parents are also transnational adoptions (Evan B. Donaldson Institute 2002; U.S. Department of State 2001). In 2002, three-fourths of all transnational adoptions were from one of five countries: China, Russia, South Korea, Guatemala, and Ukraine. Some argue that such adoptions support the blurring of racial and ethnic boundaries and expand the reality of a multicultural and color-blind world. Examination of intercountry adoption data demonstrate, however, that in the past ten years children from the top five sending countries are located in Bonilla-Silva's white and honorary white racial categories. A quarter of all U.S. international adoptions come from China and rates of adoption from the Ukraine and Russia have increased rapidly, with 50,000 of 139,000 transnational adoptees emerging from one of these two countries in the past ten years. C. Gailey's (1999) ethnography of North American adoptive families is instructive, as Gailey found "Blue Ribbon Babies" (i.e., healthy white infants from other countries) the desired commodity by these couples who were also predisposed to accept stories of birth parents and families as abusive or negligent.

With the changing and dominant definition of transracial by the adoption arena now referring to black and biracial domestic adoption, the majority of transnational adoptions are not transracial adoptions. Certainly, the poorest continent in the world, Africa, has typically had little to no participation in intercountry adoption. Extending this examination to the past twenty years of intercountry adoption data reveals the majority of transnational adoptions contribute to reconfiguring race in the United States along the lines of Bonilla-Silva's new racial typology (2001).

Results are mixed regarding racialization, and research suggests that racial identification changes with age; however, there is support for the argument that transnational adoption is effective in creating honorary members of the dominant society, as transnational adoptees are "highly acculturated" to the dominant culture (R. Lee 2003). Transnational adoption challenges racialized power structures only when these adoptions are also transracial. To be clear, it is not the intentions of adoptive couples that are at issue, but rather the outcomes for children. Individual children are "rescued" in association with their racialized position in the United States (and increasingly the worldwide racial structure). This occurs at the cost of not only children with darker skin, but all children similarly situated, as lack of state interventions in remediating poverty and disrupting families is sanctioned in favor of entitling market mechanisms and the countries these markets serve. Intercountry/transnational adoption, whether by design or default, has become part of the reconfiguring of race and of the "global hegemonic project."

PRIVATE DOMESTIC ADOPTION

Implementing standards for intercountry adoption may have positive effects for domestic adoption practices. However, this remains to be seen, and without a comparable set of standards for domestic adoption, it is impossible to assess practices or abuses occurring in private adoption agencies. Federal and state subsidies and medical assistance to adoptive families have promoted adoption of children with special needs and resulted in increased rates of special needs adoptions. Reporting results of a 1993 study, the North American Council on Adoptable Children (2002) estimated relative savings to federal and state governments at over $1 billion in administrative costs for foster care (1983–1987). A more recent study estimated adoption of 40,000 foster care children would save the federal government anywhere from $3.3 billion to $6.3 billion (Barth et al. 2006). However, efforts to promote adoption from foster care carry risks as well as potential savings. For example, in Kentucky, complaints were made that parent rights had been prematurely terminated in order to increase adoptions from the foster care system and with them federal funds (National Institute on Children, Youth & Families, Inc. 2006). Despite efforts to increase adoptions from public agencies, a substantial number of children remain in the system, and recent cuts in state subsidies could result in stagnation of adoptions (Gibbs et al. 2006).

At the same time that special needs and intercountry adoptions have increased, the number of African American children placed with families from other countries (Canada, France, Germany, the Netherlands) has also increased. Black birth mothers who work with private agencies and select couples from abroad are an important part of this process; however, private adoption and American demand has, in Patricia Williams's words, turned "being black into an actual birth defect" (2003, 165). A number of newspaper and magazine articles have suggested that at least one motivation for placement abroad is an assumption that racism is less virulent in European countries and Canada.

In our new global reality, there ought to be a focus on improving the living conditions of children both here and abroad. Measures should be put in place to assure that money gained through private and intercountry adoption is used to improve conditions for families in developing countries, with a focus on sustaining families rather than adopting their children. In addition to ratification and implementation of standards for intercountry adoptions, a central authority comparable to the State Department is needed to accredit, monitor, and report on adoption of American children through private agencies. This authority should publish regular reports on private-agency practice for the protection of children and adoptive parents. In an ideal world, adoption would not be needed, and certainly in a color-blind world, seven of ten adopters would not be white.

Adoption experts have called for broadening adoption policies and reeducating the public and adoption professionals. Despite the claim that fewer children are available in the United States, the real issue seems to be which children adoptive parents want. A broader definition of who can adopt (gays, singles, older couples) needs to be embraced and not just for special needs cases. The relationship between Judeo-Christian beliefs and attitudes toward gay and lesbian persons coupled with the current conservative backlash in America has resulted in new attempts to delimit adoption boundaries. Determining who can adopt is subject to states', agencies', and individual social workers' interpretations of adoption policy, as adoption practices vary widely. For example, Arizona has been working on legislation to ban adoptions by gays and give preference to married couples, thereby making adoption by single persons difficult, if not impossible. Single persons are also directed toward adoption of special needs children. Certainly children with special needs require loving homes, and people should be encouraged to adopt these children. However, just as program requirements are more lax for adoption of minority children, older persons/couples and gay/lesbian parents are often regarded as second- or third-rate families, so special-needs adoptions are allowed and even encouraged for these groups.

How do we address adoptions of American children by persons/couples from other countries? Just as limits are placed on who gets in (it is much more difficult to adopt infants and children from Mexico than from China), we should also have limits on placing American children out of country. Of course, it is important to honor the decisions of birth mothers and provide children opportunities in life, but this involves risks similar to those in inter-country adoption and begs the question of which children will be promoted for intercountry adoption.

During her adoption journey, Patricia Williams was asked, "What races would you accept?" She wondered, "Would they truly consider placing 'any' child with me if this agency happened to have a 'surplus' of white babies? Would I get a Korean baby if I asked? And for all the advertised difficulties, what does it mean that it is so relatively easy for white American families not just to adopt black children but to choose from a range of colors, nationalities, and configurations from around the world?" (2003, 161). Parallel to Trenka's assessment of intercountry adoption, Williams argued that the fact that blacks are materially advantaged by living in white families should direct attention to the redistribution of resources so that African Americans and all parents can afford to raise their children rather than place them for transracial or minority adoption.

Perhaps nowhere more than in private adoption does the sociopolitical category of race collapse perfectly into the private sphere, where a discourse of consumerism and agency predominate and even dictate the rules for interaction. In a color-blind society where race is now supposedly only as important as one allows it to be, private agency websites contradict the discourse of color blindness and offer racialized presentations and prices in the marketplace of infants and children. The language and public presentation of private adoption agencies represents more than a mode of communication. They are also sites of struggle, naming, organizing, and defining difference in a shifting but recalcitrant racial hierarchy. Changes in adoption discourse show how race is not simply a static concept but an interactive and dynamic one for some groups more than for others. Of course, in a color-blind world, categories such as Minority, African American, and Biracial would not be necessary or desired. It is unfortunate yet obvious that race matters in private adoption simply because it continues to matter outside of adoption, in America.

NOTE

1. According to the Evan B. Donaldson Adoption Institute (2002), at the end of the 1990s, there were 80 U.S. agencies in Russia and 150 in China.

References

ABC World News. 2005. "Foreigners Vie to Adopt Black U.S. Babies." *ABC World News*, March 5, 2005. www.abcnews.go.com/search?searchtext=foreigners%20 Vie%20Adopt%20black (accessed May 19, 2005).

Abma, J. C., A. Chandra, W. D. Mosher, L. S. Peterson, and L. J. Piccinino. 1997. "Fertility, Family Planning and Women's Health: New Data from the 1995 National Survey of Family Growth." *Vital Health Statistics* 23, no. 19: 1–35.

Adamec, C., and W. Pierce. *The Encylopedia of Adoption*. 2nd ed. New York: Facts on File, 2000.

Administration for Children and Families (ACF). 2005. "Children in Public Foster Care Waiting to Be Adopted: FY 1999 thru FY 2003." www.acf.hhs.gov/programs/ cb/stats_research/afcars/waiting2003.htm (accessed August 5, 2003).

Adoption and Foster Care Analysis and Reporting System. U.S. Department of Health and Human Services, Administration for Children and Family, Administration on Children, Youth and Families, Children's Bureau. "Trends in Foster Care and Adoption as of 11/01/02." www.acf.hhs.gov/programs/cb/dis/ afcars/publications/afcars.htm (accessed August 5, 2003).

Adoption Glossary and Termnology. 2005. http://www.glossary.adoption.com (accessed February 13, 2006).

Alexander, R., and C. M. Curtis. 1996. "A Review of Empirical Research Involving the Transracial Adoption of African American Children." *Journal of Black Psychology*, 22: 223–35.

Ansell, A. 1997. *New Right, New Racism: Race and Reaction in the United States and Britain*. New York: New York University Press.

Bacharach, C. A., K. London, and P. Maza. 1991. "On the Path to Adoption: Adoption Seeking in the United States, 1988." *Journal of Marriage and the Family* 53: 705–18.

Banks, R. R. 1998. "The Color of Desire: Fulfilling Adoptive Parents' Racial Preferences through Discriminatory State Action." *Yale Law Journal* 107: 875–964.

Barlow, A. *Between Fear and Hope: Globalization and Race in the United States*. Lanham, MD: Rowman & Littlefield, 2003

Barth, R., C. K. Lee, J. Wildfire, and S. Guo. 2006. "A Comparison of the Governmental Costs of Long-Term Foster Care and Adoption." *Social Service Review* 80, no. 1: 127–58.

Bartholet, E. 1991. "Where Do Black Children Belong? The Politics of Race Matching in Adoption." *University of Pennsylvania Law Review* 139: 1163–1256.

———. 1999. *Nobody's Children*. Boston: Beacon Press.

Berebitsky, J. 2000. *Like Our Very Own: Adoption and the Changing Culture of Motherhood, 1851–1950*. Lawrence: University Press of Kansas, 2000.

Berkeley, K. 1999. *The Women's Liberation Movement in America*. Westport, CT: Greenwood Press.

Berry, M. F. 1996. "Vindicating Martin Luther King, Jr.: The Road to a Color-Blind Society." *The Journal of Negro History* 81, nos. 1–4: 137–43.

Best-Hopkins, M. 1997. *Toddler Adoption*. Indianapolis, IN: Perspectives Press.

Billingsley, A., and J. M. Giovannoni. 1972. *Children of the Storm*. New York: Harcourt Brace Jovanovich.

Blum, L. A. 2002. *"I'm Not a Racist, but . . .": The Moral Quandary of Race*. Ithaca, NY: Cornell University Press.

Bobo, L. 2004. "Inequalities that Endure? Racial Ideology, American Politics, and the Peculiar Role of the Social Sciences." Pp. 13–42 in *The Changing Terrain of Race and Ethnicity*, ed. M. Krysan and A. E. Lewis. New York: Russell Sage Foundation.

Bobo, L., and J. R. Kluegel. 1997. "Status, Ideology, and Dimensions of Whites' Racial Beliefs and Attitudes: Progress and Stagnation." Pp. 93–120 in *Racial Attitudes in the 1990s: Continuity and Change*, ed. S. Tuch and J. Martin. Westport, CT: Praeger, 1997.

Bobo, L., J. R. Kluegel, and R. A. Smith. 1997. "Laissez-Faire Racism: The Crystallization of a Kinder, Gentler Anti-Black Ideology." Pp. 15–42 in *Racial Attitudes in the 1990s: Continuity and Change*, ed. S. Tuch and J. Martin. Westport, CT: Praeger.

Boger, J. C., and G. Orfield. 2006. *School Resegregation: Must the South Turn Back?* Chapel Hill: University of North Carolina Press, 2006.

Bonilla-Silva, E. 2001. *White Supremacy and Racism in the Post–Civil Rights Era.* Boulder, CO: Lynne Rienner.

———. 2003. *Racism without Racists.* Lanham, MD: Rowman & Littlefield.

Bonilla-Silva, E., and T. Forman. 2000. "'I'm Not a Racist, but . . .': Mapping White College Students' Racial Ideology in the U.S." *Discourse and Society* 11, no. 1: 50–85.

Bonilla-Silva, E., and K. Glover. 2004. "We Are All Americans: The Latin Americanization of Race Relations in the United States." Pp. 149–86 in *The Changing Terrain of Race & Ethnicity*, ed. M. Krysan and A. E. Lewis. New York: Russell Sage Foundation.

Bordia, P. 1996. "Studying Verbal Interaction on the Internet: The Case of Rumor Transmission Research." *Behavior Research Methods, Instruments and Computers* 28, no. 2: 149–51.

Bradley, C., and C. G. Hawkins-Leon. 2002. "The Transracial Adoption Debate: Counseling and Legal Implications." *Journal of Counseling and Development* 80, no. 4 (2002): 433–442.

Brown, M. K., M. Carnoy, E. Currie, T. Duster, D. B. Oppenheimer, M. M. Shultz, and D. Wellman. 2003. *Whitewashing Race: The Myth of a Color-Blind Society.* Berkeley: University of California Press.

Brunsma D. L. 2006. "Mixed Messages: Doing Race in a 'Color-Blind' Era." In *Mixed Messages: Multiracial Identities in the 'Color-Blind' Era*, ed. D. L. Brunsma. Boulder, CO: Lynne Rienner Publishers.

Carp, E. W., ed. 2002. *Adoption in America*. Ann Arbor: University of Michigan Press.

Center for Adoptee Rights. 2003. *Adoption-Speak*. http://www.netaxs.com/~sparky/adoption/aspeak.htm (accessed March 14, 2005).

Chandra, A., J. Abma, P. Maza, and C. Bachrach. 1999. "Adoption, Adoption Seeking, and Relinquishment for Adoption in the United States." *Advance Data* 306. Washington, D.C.: Centers for Disease Control and Prevention/National Center for Health Statistics. http://www.cdc.gov/nchs/data/ad/ad306.pdf.

Conley, D. 1999. *Being Black, Living in the Red: Race, Wealth, and Social Policy in America*. Berkeley: University of California Press.

Courtney, M. E. 1997. "The Politics and Realities of Transracial Adoption." *Child Welfare* 76, no. 6: 749–80.

Cox, S. S-K. 1999. *Voices from Another Place: A Collection of Works from a Generation Born in Korea and Adopted to Other Countries*. St. Paul: Yeong & Yeong.

Cremin, L. 1988. *American Education: The Metropolitan Experience, 1876–1980*. New York: HarperCollins.

Crenshaw, K. 1997. "Color-Blind Dreams and Racial Nightmares: Reconfiguring Racism in the Post–Civil Rights Era." Pp. 97–168 in *Birth of a Nation'hood*, ed. T. Morrison and C. B. Lacour. New York: Pantheon Books.

Davis, F. J. 1991. *Who Is Black? One Nation's Definition*. University Park: Pennsylvania State University Press.

DiTomaso, N., R. Parks-Yancy, and C. Post. 2003. "White Views of Civil Rights: Color Blindness and Equal Opportunity." Pp. 189–98 in *White Out*, ed. A.W. Doane and E. Bonilla-Silva. New York: Routledge.

Doane, A. W. 2003. "Rethinking Whiteness Studies." Pp. 3–20 in *White Out: The Continuing Significance of Racism*, ed. A. Doane and E. Bonilla-Silva. New York: Routledge.

D'Souza, D. 1995. *The End of Racism*. New York: Free Press.

Ebert, K. 2004. "Demystifying Color-Blind Ideology: Denying Race, Ignoring Racial Inequalities." Pp. 174–96 in *Skin/Deep: How Race and Complexion Matter in the "Color-Blind" Era*, ed. C. Herring, V. M. Keith, and H. D. Horton. Chicago: University of Illinois Press.

Ehrenreich, B., and A. R. Hochschild. 2002. *Global Woman: Nannies, Maids, and Sex Workers in the New Economy.* New York: Owl Books.

Emerson, M., G. Yancey, and K. Chai. 2001. "Does Race Matter in Residential Segregation? Exploring the Preferences of White Americans." *American Sociological Review* 66: 922–35.

Evan B. Donaldson Adoption Institute. 2002. "International Adoption Facts." http://www.adoptioninstitute.org/FactOverview/international.html (accessed January 7, 2004).

Fancott, H. 1997. *Unwanted Adoption Language.* Adoptive Families Association of BC. http://www.bcadoption.com/articles/aam/lang.htm (accessed March 14, 2005).

Farley, R., C. Steeh, M. Krysan, T. Jackson, and K. Reeves. 1994. "Stereotypes and Segregation: Neighborhoods in the Detroit Area." *American Journal of Sociology* 100: 750–80.

Feagin, J. 2003. *White Men on Race: Power, Privilege, and the Shaping of Cultural Consciousness.* Boston: Beacon Press.

Feagin, J., and H. Vera. 1995. *White Racism: The Basics.* New York: Routledge.

Fisher, A. 2003. "Still 'Not Quite as Good as Having Your Own'? Toward a Sociology of Adoption." *Annual Review of Sociology* 29: 335–55.

Fonseca, C. 2003a. "Transracial Connections and Dissenting Views: Intercountry Adoption in Brazil." Unpublished paper.

———. 2003b. "Patterns of Shared Parenthood among the Brazilian Poor." *Social Text*, special issue on transnational adoption, edited by T. Volkman and C. Katz: 111–27.

Freeman, J. 1982. *Social Movements of the Sixties and Seventies.* United Kingdom: Longman.

Fregoso, R. L. 2003. *Mexicana Encounters: The Making of Social Identities on the Borderlands.* Berkeley: University of California Press.

Freidmutter, C. 2002. "International Adoptions: Problems and Solutions." Testimony before the House Committee on International Relations, May 22. www.adoptioninstitute.org/policy/hagueregs.html (accessed February 16, 2006).

Freundlich, M. 1998. "Supply and Demand: The Forces Shaping the Future of Adoption." *Adoption Quarterly* 2, no. 1: 13–46.

——. 2000a. *The Market Forces in Adoption.* Washington, DC: Child Welfare League of America/The Evan B. Donaldson Adoption Institute.

——. 2000b. *The Role of Race, Culture, and National Origin in Adoption.* Washington, DC: Child Welfare League of American/Evan B. Donaldson Institute.

Freundlich, M., and Lieberthal, J. K. "The Gathering of the First Generation of Adult Korean Adoptees: Adoptees' Perceptions of International Adoption." www.adoptioninstitute.org (accessed November 21, 2002).

Gailey, C. W. 1999. "Seeking 'Baby Right': Race, Class, and Gender in US International Adoption". Pp. 52–80 in *Mine, Yours, Ours . . . and Theirs: Adoption, Changing Kinship and Family Patterns,* ed. A. L. Rygvold, M. Dalen, and B. Saetersdal. Oslo, Norway: University of Oslo.

Gallagher, C. 2003. "Color-Blind Privilege: The Social and Political Functions of Erasing the Color Line in Post-Race America." *Race, Gender and Class* 10, no. 4: 1–17.

Gallup Organization. 2001. *Black and White Relations in the United States: Update, Special Reports.* July.

Gibbs, D., B. Dalberth, N. Berkman, and D. Weitzenkamp. 2006. "Determinants of Adoption Subsidies." *Adoption Quarterly* 9, nos. 2–3: 63–80.

Gill, B. 2002. "Adoption Agencies and the Search for the Ideal Family." Pp. 160–80 in *Adoption in America,* ed. E. W. Carp. Ann Arbor: University of Michigan Press.

Giroux, H. A. 2006. "Spectacles of Race and Pedagogies of Denial: Anti-Black Racist Pedagogy." Pp. 68–93 in *The Globalization of Racism,* ed. D. Macedo and P. Gounari. Boulder, CO: Paradigm Publishers.

Goldberg, D. T. 2002. *The Racial State.* Malden, MA: Blackwell Publishers.

Gómez-Peña, G. 2003. "A Postdemocratic Era." Pp. 415–416 in *Latino/a Thought: Culture, Politics and Society,* ed. F. H. Vazquez and R. D. Torres. New York: Rowman & Littlefield Publishers.

Gordon, L. 1999. *The Great Arizona Orphan Abduction.* Cambridge, MA: Harvard University Press.

Frankenberg, R. 1993. *White Women, Race Matters: The Social Construction of Whiteness*. Minneapolis: University of Minnesota Press.

Harris Interactive, Inc. 2002 *National Adoption Attitudes Survey*. Evan B. Donaldson Adoption Institute. www.adoptioninstitute.org/survey/Adoption_Exec_Summ.pdf (accessed February 16, 2005).

Herman, E. N.d. *The Adoption History Project*. http://darkwing.uoregon.edu/~adoption/siteindex.html (accessed November 16, 2004; February 15, 2005).

———. 2002. "The Paradoxical Rationalization of Modern Adoption." *Journal of Social History* 36 (Winter): 339–85.

Herring, C. H. 2004. *Skin/Deep: How Race and Complexion Matter in the "Color-Blind Era."* Urbana and Chicago: University of Illinois Press.

Hine C. 2000. *Virtual Ethnography*. London: Sage Publications.

Hollingsworth, L. D. 1998. "Promoting Same-Race Adoption for Children of Color." *Social Work* 43, no. 2: 104–16.

———. 2000. "Sociodemographic Influences in the Prediction of Attitudes Toward Transracial Adoption." *Families in Society* (January/Febuary).

Hudson, J. B., and B. M. Hines-Hudson. 1999. "A Study of the Contemporary Racial Attitudes of Whites and African Americans." *The Western Journal of Black Studies* 23, no. 22: 1–12.

Hunt, M. O. 2001. "Self-Evaluation and Stratification Beliefs." Pp. 330–50 in *Extending Self-Esteem Theory and Research: Sociological and Psychological Currents*, ed. T. J. Owens, S. Stryker, and N. Goodman. New York: Cambridge University Press.

Hunt, M. O., P. B. Jackson, B. Powell, and L. C. Steelman. 2000. "Color-Blind: The Treatment of Race and Ethnicity in Social Psychology." *Social Psychology Quarterly* 63: 352–64.

Hunter, M. 2005. *Race, Gender, and the Politics of Skin Tone*. New York: Routledge.

International Organization for Migration. N.d. *Trafficking for Sexual Exploitation: The Case of the Russian Federation*. New York: United Nations.

Jacoby, T. 1998. *Someone Else's House: America's Unfinished Struggle for Integration*. New York: Free Press.

Johnson, H. B., and T. M. Shapiro. 2003. "Good Neighbors, Good Schools: Race and the 'Bood Choices' of White Families." Pp. 173–88 in *White Out: The Continuing Significance of Racism*, ed. A. Doane and E. Bonilla-Silva. New York: Routledge.

Johnston, P. I. 2001. *Adoption Is a Family Affair! What Relatives and Friends Must Know*. Indianapolis, IN: Perspectives Press.

——. 2004. "Speaking Positively: An Introduction to Respectful Adoption Language." http://www.perspectivespress.com (accessed November 8, 2004).

Kaiser Foundation. 2001. *Race and Ethnicity in 2001: Attitudes, Perceptions and Experiences*. Washington DC: Kaiser Family Foundation.

Kennedy, R. 2003. *Interracial Intimacies: Sex, Marriage, Identity and Adoption*. New York: Pantheon Books.

Kim, E. 2000. *Ten Thousand Sorrows*. New York: Doubleday.

Kline, W. 2001. *Building a Better Race: Gender, Sexuality, and Eugenics from the Turn of the Century to the Baby Boom*. Berkeley: University of California Press.

Kozol, J. 2005. *The Shame of the Nation: The Restoration of Apartheid Schooling in America*. New York: Crown Publishers.

Krysan, M. 2002a. "Community Undesirability in Black and White: Examining Racial Residential Preferences through Community Perceptions." *Social Problems* 49: 521–43.

——. 2002b. "Whites Who Say They'd Flee: Who Are They, and Why Would They Leave?" *Demography* 39: 675–96.

Ladner, J. A. 1977. *Mixed Families: Adopting Across Racial Boundaries*. New York: Anchor Books..

Lee, J. L., and F. D. Bean. 2003. "Beyond Black and White: Remaking Race in America." *Context* 2, no. 3: 26–33.

Lee, R. 2003. "The Transracial Adoption Paradox: History, Research and Counseling Implications of Cultural Socialization." *Counseling Psychologist* 31: 711–42.

——. "The Coming of Age of Korean Adoptees: Ethnic Identity Development and Psychological Adjustiment." Pp. 203–38 in *Korean-Americans: Past, Present and Future*, ed. I. J. Kim. Elizabeth, NJ: Hollym International Corporation.

Lewis, A. E. 2001. "There Is No 'Race' in the Schoolyard: Colorblind Ideology in an (Almost) All-White School." *American Educational Research Journal* 38, no. 4: 781–812.

Lewis, A. E., et al. 2004. 2004. "Institutional Patterns and Transformations: Race and Ethnicity in Housing, Education, Labor Markets, Religion, and Criminal Justice." Pp. 67–119 in *The Changing Terrain of Race and Ethnicity*, ed. M. Krysan and A. E. Lewis. New York: Russell Sage Foundation.

Lieberthal, J. K. 2001. "Adoption in the Absence of National Boundaries." Presentation at 25th Conference of the North American Council on Adoptable Children. Evan B. Donaldson Adoption Institute. http:www.adoptioninstitute .org.policy/staff.html (accessed September 22, 2003).

Lindemeyer, K. 1997. *A Right to Childhood: The U.S. Children's Bureau and Child Welfare, 1912–1946*. Urbana: University of Illinois Press.

Logan, E. N.d. "The Politics of Colorblind Advocacy of Transracial Adoption: Race, History, Power and Community." Unpublished manuscript. Department of Sociology, University of Minnesota, Minneapolis.

Macedo, D., and L. I. Bartolome. 2001. *Dancing with Bigotry: Beyond the Politics of Tolerance*. Palgrave Macmillan.

MacLean, N. 2006. *Freedom Is Not Enough*. Cambridge, MA: Harvard University Press.

Mahoney, J. 1991. "The Black Baby Doll: Transracial Adoption and Cultural Preservation." *University of Missouri Kansas City Law Review*, 59: 487–501.

Mansnerus, L. 1998. "Market Puts Price Tags on the Priceless." *New York Times*, October 28, A1, A16–A17.

Marindin, H., ed. 1992. *Handbook for Single Adoptive Parents*. Washington, DC: National Council for Single Adoptive Parents.

Massey, D., and N. Denton. 1993. *American Apartheid: Segregation and the Making of the Underclass*. Cambridge, MA: Harvard University Press.

Massey, D., and M. J. Fisher. 1999. "Does Rising Income Bring Integration? New Results for Blacks, Hispanics, and Asians in 1990." *Social Science Research* 28, no. 3: 316–26.

Masson, J. 2001. "Intercountry Adoption: A Global Problem or a Global Solution?" *Journal of International Affairs* 55, no. 1: 141–54.

May, E. T. 1995. *Barren in the Promised Land: Childless Americans and the Pursuit of Happiness*. New York: Basic Books.

McIntosh, P. 1989. "White Priviledge: Unpacking the Invisible Knapsack." *Peace and Freedom* (July/August): 10-12.

McKinnon, C. 1989. *Toward a Feminist Theory of the State*. Cambridge, MA: Harvard University Press.

McRoy, R. G. 1989. "An Organizational Dilemma: The Case of Transracial Adoptions. *Journal of Applied Behavior Science* 25: 145–60.

Melina, L. R. 1989. *Making Sense of Adoption: A Parent's Guide*. New York: Harper Publishers.

Melosh, B. 2002. *Strangers and Kin: The American Way of Adoption*. Cambridge, MA: Harvard University Press.

Modell, J., and N. Dambacher. 1997. "Making a 'Real' Family: Matching and Cultural Biologism in American Adoption." *Adoption Quarterly* 1, no. 2: 3–33.

Modell, J. S. 2002. *A Sealed and Sacred Kinship: The Culture of Policies and Practices in American Adoption*. New York: Berghahn.

Morrison, T., ed. 1992. "Introduction." In *Race-ing Justice, Engendering Power: Essays on Anita Hill, Clarence Thomas and the Construction of Social Reality*. New York: Pantheon Books.

National Adoption Information Clearinghouse (NAIC). 2002. "Adoption Statistics: A Brief Overview of the Data." http://www.calib.com/naic/stats/index.cfm and http://naic.acf.hhas.gov/pubs/twenty.cfm (accessed August 5, 2003).

———. 2003. "Intercountry Adoption." (accessed August 5, 2003).

———. 2004a. "How Many Children Were Adopted in 2000 and 2001?" http://naic.acf.hhs.gov/pubs/four.cfm (accessed January 10, 2004).

———. 2004b. "U.S. Children Placed for Adoption with non-U.S. Citizens." http://naic.acf.hhs.gov/pubs/s_adopted/index.cfm (accessed January 10, 2004).

National Center for Health Statistics. 1997. "Fertility, Family Planning, and Women's Health: New Data from the 1995 National Survey of Family Growth." *Vital Health Statistics* 23, no. 19. www.cdc.gov/nchs/data/series/sr_23/sr23_019.pdf.

National Institute on Children, Youth & Families, Inc. 2006. "The 'Other' Kentucky Lottery: Child Protection and Permanency for Abused and Neglected Children in

Kentucky in 2005." National Institute on Children, Youth & Families, Inc., and Kentucky Youth Advocates, Inc.

North American Council on Adoptable Children. 2002. "Adoption Subsidies as an Affordable Option." http://www.nacac.org/subsidyfactsheets/affordable.html (accessed July 26, 2006).

Ó Dochartaigh, N. 2002. *The Internet Research Handbook*. London: Sage Publications.

Oliver, M. L., and T. M. Shapiro. 1997. *Black Wealth/White Wealth: A New Perspective on Racial Inequality*. New York: Routledge.

Omi, M., and H. Winant. 1994. *Racial Formation in the United States*. New York: Routledge.

Orfield, G., and C. Ashkinaze. 1991. *The Closing Door: Conservative Policy and Black Opportunity*. Chicago: University of Chicago Press.

Orfield, G., and S. Eaton. 1997. *Dismantling Desegregation: The Quiet Reversal of Brown v. Board of Education*. New York: New Press.

Ortiz, A.T. and L. Briggs. 2003. "The Culture of Poverty, Crack Babies, and Welfare Cheats: The Making of the 'Healthy White Baby Crisis." *Social Text*, 39–57

Pattilo-McCoy, M. 1999. *Black Picket Fences*. Chicago: University of Chicago Press.

Patton, S. 2000. *Birth Marks: Transracial Adoption in Contemporary America*. New York: New York University Press.

Perry, T. 1994. "The Transracial Adoption Controversy: An Analysis of Discourse and Subordination." *NYU Review of Law and Social Change* 21, no. 3: 34–107.

———. 1998. "Transracial and International Adoption: Mothers, Hierarchy, Race and Feminist Legal Theory." *Yale Journal of Law and Feminism* 10: 101–64.

Pertman, A. 2000. *Adoption Nation: How the Adoption Revolution is Transforming America*. New York: Basic Books.

Platt, A. 1997. "The Land That Never Has Been Yet: U.S. Race Relations at the Crossroads." *Journal of Social Justice* 24, no. 1.

Pollock, M. 2004. *Colormute: Race Talk Dilemmas in an American School*. Princeton, NJ: Princeton University Press.

Princeton Survey Research Associates. 1997. *Benchmark Adoption Survey: Report on the Findings*. http://www.adoptioninstitute.org/survey/Benchmark_Survey_1997.pdf (accessed January 5, 2006).

Roberts, D. 2002. *Shattered Bonds: The Color of Welfare.* New York: Basic Books.

Rothman, B. K. 2005. *Weaving a Family.* Boston: Beacon Press.

Sallee, S. 2004. *The Whiteness of Child Labor Reform in the New South.* Athens: University of Georgia Press.

Schuman, H., C. Steeh, L. Bobo, and M. Krysan. 1997. *Racial Attitudes in America.* Cambridge, MA: Harvard University Press.

Sears, D. 1988. "Symbolic Racism." Pp. 53–84 in *Eliminating Racism: Profiles in Controversy,* ed. P. Katz and D. Taylor. New York: Plenum.

Sears, D., J. Sidanius, and L. Bobo. 2001. *Racialized Politics: The Debate about Racism in America.* Chicago: University of Chicago Press.

Selman, P. 2001. "Intercountry Adoption in the New Millennium: The 'Quiet' Migration Revisited." Paper presented at the European Population Conference, Helsinki, Finland.

Shapiro, T. M. 2004. *The Hidden Cost of Being African American: How Wealth Perpetuates Inequality.* New York: Oxford University Press.

Shipler, D. A. 1998. *Country of Strangers: Blacks and Whites in America.* New York: Vintage Books.

Simon, R., and H. Altstein. 1977. *Transracial Adoption.* New York: John Wiley & Sons.

Sklair, L. 2004. "Sociology of the Global System." Pp. 70–75 in *The Globalization Reader,* ed. F. J. Lechner and J. Boli. United Kingdom: Blackwell Publishing.

Sleeper, J. 1997. *Liberal Racism.* New York: Penguin Books.

Smith, E. P., and L. A. Merkel-Holguin. 1995. *A History of Child Welfare.* New Brunswick, NJ: Transaction Publishers.

Smolin, David M. 2005. "Child Laundering: How the Intercountry Adoption System Legitimizes and Incentivizes the Practices of Buying, Trafficking, Kidnapping, and Stealing Children." bepress Legal Repository. http://law.bepress.com/expresso/eps/749 (accessed January 5, 2006).

Solinger, R. 1992. *Wake Up Little Susie: Single Pregnancy and Race before* Roe v. Wade. New York: Routledge.

———. 2001. *Beggars and Choosers: How the Politics of Choice Shapes Adoption, Abortion, and Welfare.* New York: Hill and Wang.

Stack, C. 1974. *All Our Kin: Strategies for Survival in a Black Community.* New York: Harper Colophon.

Tarmann, A. 2007. "International Adoption Rate in U.S. Doubled in the 1990s." www.prb.org/articles/2003/InternationalAdoptionRateinUSDoubledinthe1990s.

Taylor, M. 1998. "How Whites' Racial Attitudes Vary with the Racial Composition of Local Populations: Numbers Count." *American Sociological Review* 63: 512–35.

Thernstrom, S., and A. Thernstrom. 1999. *America in Black and White: One Nation, Indivisible.* New York: Simon & Schuster.

Trenka, J. J. 2003. *The Language of Blood: A Memoir.* St. Paul: Borealis Books.

———. 2005. "Whywrite." http://www.languageofblood.com/whywrite.html (accessed July 9, 2006).

Trenka, J. J., C. Oparah, and S. Y. Shin, eds. 2006. *Outsiders Within: Writing on Transracial Adoption.* Cambridge, MA: South End Press.

UNICEF. N.d. "Inter-country Adoption." UNICEF. http://www.unicef.org/media/ media_15011.html. (accessed July 21, 2006).

U.S. Department of Health and Human Services. 2000. *The AFCARS Report: Current Estimates as of January 2000.* Washington, DC: U.S. Department of Health and Human Services, Administration for Children and Families.

———. 2004. *Child Welfare Outcomes 2001: Annual Report.* Washington, DC: Department of Health and Human Services.

U.S. Department of State. 2001. Immigrant Visas Issued to Orphans Coming to the U.S., FY 1989-2001. http://travel.state.gov/orphan_numbers.html (accessed November 21, 2002).

———. 2005a. "Immigrant Visas Issued to Orphans Coming to the U.S." Travel.State.Gov. http://travel.state.gov/family/adoption/stats/ stats_451.html (accessed February 18, 2006).

———. 2005b. *Summary Data: Immediate Relative Visas Issued, FY 1991–FY 2001.* http://travel.state.gov/orphan_numbers.html (accessed February 18, 2006).

Vieni, M. 1975. "Transracial Adoption Is a Solution Now." *Social Work* 20: 419–21.

Warschauer, M. 2000. "Language, Identity and the Internet." Pp 151–70 in *Race in Cyberspace*, eds. B. E. Kolko, L. Nakamura, and G. B. Rodman. New York: Routledge.

Wegar, K. 1997. *Adoption, Identity, and Kinship*. New Haven, CT: Yale University Press.

Weiss, A. 2006. "The Racism of Globalization." Pp. 128–47 in *The Globalization of Racism*, ed. D. Macedo and P. Gounari. Boulder, CO: Paradigm Publishers.

Williams, P. 2003. "Spare Parts, Family Values, Old Children, Cheap." Pp. 159–66 in *Critical Race Feminism*, ed. A. D. Wing. New York: New York University Press.

Wilson, T. 1996. "Cohort and Prejudice: Whites' Attitudes toward Blacks, Hispanics, Jews, and Asians." *Public Opinions Quarterly* 60: 253–74.

Winant, H. 2004. *The New Politics of Race*. Minneapolis: University of Minnesota Press.

Working, R., and A. Madhani. 2003. "Parents Often Not Ready for Needy Foreign Kids." *Chicago Tribune*, December 28.

Wulczyn, F., K. Hislop, and L. Chen. 2005. "Adoption Dynamics: An Update on the Impact of the Adoption and Safe Families Act." Working paper, University of Chicago, Chapin Hall Center for Children.

Yancey, G. 2003. *Who Is White? Latinos, Asians, and the New Black/Nonblack Divide*. Boulder, CO: Lynne Rienner Publishers.

———. 2006. "Racial Justice in a Black/Nonblack Society." In *Mixed Messages: Multiracial Identities in the 'Color-Blind' Era*, ed. D. L. Brunsma. Boulder, CO: Lynne Reinner Publishers.

Yinger, J. 1995. *Closed Doors, Opportunities Lost*. New York: Russell Sage Foundation.

Zeliger, V. 1985. *Pricing the Priceless Child: The Changing Social Value of Children*. Princeton, NJ: Princeton University Press.

Index

Pages in italics refer to illustrations.

Adoption Advantage agency, 71–72
Adoption and Foster Care Analysis and
  Reporting System. *See* AFCARS
Adoption and Safe Families Act (AFSA),
  67. *See also* federal and state subsidies
Adoption.com, 55, 59–62
adoption data collection, 10–11, 55
adoption forums: Adoption.com, 86; *Ask
  the Experts*, 87. *See also* New York
  State Citizens' Coalition for Children,
  106
"Adoption Glossary and Terminology,"
  30, 43
Adoption History Project, The, 30
adoption industry: impact on shaping
  parent choice, 51
Adoption Is a Family Affair (Johnston),
  30, 45. *See also* popular adoption
  books
Adoption Nation (Pertman), 30, 45–46.
  See also popular adoption books

AdoptionNetwork.com, 84, *85*
adoption programs: categories on
  websites, 57–59, 60. *See also* minority
  programs
adoption requirements, 70–76
adoptions: adoption placement, 18; and
  class, 19, 23; as colonial project,
  25–26; and race, 19; and re-
  racialization of the world, 25
adoptions of African Americans: by
  African American families, 21; by
  foreigners, 4, 78–79, 116, 117–18
adoption organizations and
  foundations, 30. *See also* Evan B.
  Donaldson Institute on
Adoption Institute; National Adoption
  Information Clearinghouse; North
  American Council on Adoptable
  Children
adoption professionals, 51, 59, 64, 65,
  70, 72, 78, 94, 117

Adoption Support Center, 73

adoptive parent profiles, 83–84, *85. See also* AdoptionNetwork.com; ParentProfiles.com

advertising by private adoption agencies, 49

AFCARS (Adoption and Foster Care Analysis and Reporting System), 10, 67. *See also* adoption data collection

African American placement agencies, 29. *See also* dedicated private adoption agencies

AFSA (Adoption and Safe Families Act), 67. *See also* federal and state subsidies

age requirements, 70, 71, 73, 75

American Adoptions agency, 72

appropriateness of transracial adoption, 94–97, 106

Asian as model minority, 78; opinion polls, 6.

attitudes toward adoption, 65. *See also* National Adoption Attitudes Survey; National Survey of Family Growth

attitude surveys on race, 14. *See also* liberalization of white attitudes

availability of African American children, 63, 66, 67, 71–72, 93–94

Babies of Color (BOC), 72

Bartolome, Lilia, 30

Best-Hopkins, Mary, 46

biological racism, 15. *See also* race matching

"biracial" as descriptor, 6, 42

"Blue-Ribbon Babies," 115

BOC (Babies of Color), 72

Bonilla-Silva, Eduardo, 5, 14, 78, 111. *See also* Latin-Americanization of race; tripartite system of racial categories

Carolina Hope Christian Adoption Agency, 70–71

categories of web sites, 30. *See also* adoption programs

Catholic Charities (CC), 60, 61

Central Authority, 24; domestic adoption, 117. *See also* U.S. State Department

changes in racial identity, 103

changing definitions of children, 31

chat rooms, 86

child commerce, 22, 23, 25, 113. *See also* intercountry adoption; transnational migrants

childlessness, 31

Children of the Storm (Billingsley and Giovannoni), 18

Child Welfare League of America (CWLA), 31, *32–33*, 53

child welfare reform movement, 31

child welfare system, 18, 29, 31, *32*, 67

Chinese adoptions, 22, 78, 113, 115, 117

Chinese as almost white, 78

Civil Rights Act of 1875, 36

civil rights movement, 1, 2, 29, 36, *38–39*, 40

"clean-break" model, 23

codes: age, 66, 69; gay and lesbian, 46;. *See also* special needs; race, 43, 44, 66, 69. *See also* special needs. *See also* special needs children

"collective black" groups, 5

color-blind advocates, 15

color-blind discourse, 7

color-blind ideology, 13–14, 111

color-blind individualism, 13, 18. *See also* color-blind individualists

color-blind individualists, 3, 7

color-blind racial logic, 1. *See also* color-blind ideology; color-blind racism; laissez-faire racism; symbolic racism
color-blind racism, 13–14, 18; and civil rights movement, 15; and neoliberal racism, 13–14, 18
color consciousness, 13, 98–101
color-mute, 93
construction of "childhood," 31. *See also* changing definitions of children
constructions of children: impact on adoption, 114
Constructive Adoption Language, 41, 47
costs of adoption, 9, 64
criteria for adoption, 70–76. *See also* adoption requirements
critique of color-blind racism, 20
cross-racial children, 35, 42. *See also* transracial adoption
CWLA (Child Welfare League of America), 31, *32–33*, 53

Dancing with Bigotry (Macedo and Bartolome), 30
decline of white infants, 40, 63
dedicated private adoption agencies, 60
defining minority and transracial, 68
demand for African American children, 71–72, 80–81
demand side of adoption, 63–64. *See also* market forces of adoption
demonstrating racism in private adoption, 20
denial of race difference, 105
de-racing language, 93. *See also* race-neutral language
"diaper diaspora," 22

dilemmas of raising racial/ethnic children, 46. *See also Making Sense of Adoption*
discourse of consumerism, 118; of reverse discrimination, 41
DMOZ. *See* Open Directory Project

ECFA (Evangelical Child and Family Agency), 71
Encyclopedia of Adoption, The (Adamec and Pierce), 30, 51
estimates of transracial adoption, 106
eugenics movement, 31
Evan B. Donaldson Adoption Institute, 30, 55, 77
Evangelical Child and Family Agency (ECFA), 71
expectations of birthmothers, 70–71
explicit minority programs, 57, 58, 60

family acceptance of African American and biracial adoptees, 94–97
federal and state subsidies, 67
feeble-mindedness, 35, 42; "feebleminded" as descriptor, 42
fetal alcohol syndrome, 19, 77
"foreign" as descriptor, 42
forum participants' perceptions: of colorblindness, 104–5
foster care: explanations for growth of, 67; and federal savings of adoption, 116
Frankenberg, Ruth, 90

genetic testing, 34
Giroux, Henry, 15
global hegemonic project, 116
government agencies and private foundations, 55. *See also* Evan B.

Donaldson Adoption Institute;
    National Adoption Information
    Clearinghouse; North American
    Council on Adoptive Children; U.S.
    State Department
Great Arizona Orphan Abduction, 97

Hague Convention Treaty: purpose, 21,
    24
hair and skin, 101–2. *See also* "nappy"
Handbook for Single Adoptive Parents
    (Marindin), 51, 70
"handicapped" as descriptor, 42
Hispanic infants, 48, 69, 72, 73, 76, *85*,
    95, 102
"honorary white" status, 5, 76
hypodescent, 51. *See also* miscegenation

illegitimate children, 6, 31
immigration, 15–16
immigration marches, 111
Immigration Restriction Act, 34
inequality, individualistic interpretations
    of, 14
infertility, 71. *See also* childlessness
intercountry adoption: as alternative to
    minority programs, 77–78;
    complexities of, 77; contribution to
    the political economy, 112;
    corruption in, 113; critics of, 114;
    developmental delays of children
    from, 25, 82n9; focus of U.S. on, 113;
    risks of, 24, 77; and the tripartite
    system, 115. *See also* fetal alcohol
    syndrome; pediatric AIDS
Intercountry Adoption Act, 24
"intercountry" as descriptor, 42
"international" as descriptor, 42

Internet as deracialized environment, 109
Internet as zone of integration, 88
Internet-based studies, 11–12. *See also*
    Internet research
Internet research, 11–12, 30, 46–50,
    59–62, 83–88
interracial children, 35, 42; "interracial"
    as descriptor, 42. *See also* "biracial" as
    descriptor; racially mixed children
ironies of globalization, 21–22
Irwin, Patricia, 45

Jim Crow statutes, 21, 36, 37
Johnston, Patricia Irwin, 30

Katz Rothman, Barbara, 42

laissez-faire racism, 13–14
language of minority programs, 68
Latin-Americanization of race, 5. *See
    also* Latin-American-like; tripartite
    system of racial categories
Latin-Americanization of race and
    adoption, 76, 78
Latin-American-like, 5
Latino adoption, 71, 73, 75, 76. *See also*
    Hispanic infants
Lee, Richard, 25
legacy of slavery, 21
liberalization of white attitudes, 3, 4
life opportunities and race, 16–18. *See
    also* racial inequality
limitations of Internet research, 56,
    86–88. *See also* Internet research
Love Basket agency, 72

Macedo, Donaldo and Lilia Bartolome,
    30

MacLean, Nancy, 15
Making Sense of Adoption (Melina), 30, 45
marginalization of African Americans, 79
marital status, 70, 71
market forces of adoption, 62–67
market freedoms, 9
matching the "normal" family, 34
matching and segregation, 40
McIntosh, Peggy, 88
McKinnon, Catherine, 20
media presentations of race, 15
Melina, Lois, 45
minimum standards of adoption, 34
minority programs, 11, 46, *47*, 56, 57, 60, 61, 67–79
minority programs serving as niche market, 70
Minutemen, 14
miscegenation, 36
"mixed-race," people, 42, 91; "mixed race" as descriptor, 42
moratorium on adoption, 24
Morrison, Toni, 26
motherhood and consumerism, 42
Multi-Ethnic and Inter-Ethnic Placement Acts, 3, 5, 18, 41

"nappy," 101, 102
National Adoption Attitudes Survey, 20, 65
National Adoption Information Clearinghouse, 10, 30. *See also* adoption data collection
National Association of Black Social Workers, 3; position on transracial adoption, 19

National Center for State Courts, 10. *See also* adoption data collection
nationalism, xenophobia, and color-blind racism, 31, 111
National Survey of Family Growth, 65
Native American autonomy, 51. *See also* Multi-Ethnic and Inter-Ethnic Placement Acts
neoliberal racism, 13–14
Netscape Open Directory, 59
new challenges to the existing order, 111
new discourse of adoption, 40, 41, 42. *See also* Respectful Adoption Language
New York State Citizens' Coalition for Children (nysccc.org), 106
non-explicit minority programs, 57–58, 60
North American Council on Adoptive Children, 30, 117

Office of Immigration Statistics, 10. *See also* adoption data collection
older parents, 71, 73. *See also* age requirements
Omi, Michael and Howard Winant, 6
online adoption directories, 7, 55–69, 76
open adoption, 65, 66
Open Directory Project (DMOZ), 55, 56–58, 59, 60, 61, 69, 76. *See also* DMOZ, Netscape Open Directory
operating costs of private agencies, 64
opinion polls, 6

paradox of race, 16, 50
parent demand, 84
ParentProfiles.com, 84, *85*
Patton, Sandra, 43

pediatric AIDS, 19
persons of color as users of the Internet,
  103
Pertman, Adam, 30
pigmentocracy, 5, 78
Plan Loving's Minority Infant program,
  75
policy recommendations, 116–17
Pollack, Mica, 88
popular adoption books, 30, 44–46, 51,
  52
Positive Adoption Language, 41, *47*
potentially color-blind programs, 46, *47*,
  49, 58–59, 60
price of adoptions, 48–49, 72–74, *74–75*
private adoption agency websites, 56
private/intercountry adoption, 22
processes of racialization and choice of
  country, 115

race (defined), 20, 29
race as primary identity, 109
race-based adoption programs, 20, 49,
  67–76. *See also* types of adoption
race categories in adoption forums, 91
race-conscious policies, 2
race-loaded issues, 93
race matching, 50, 52n5, 53
race-neutral language, 13
race-neutral policy, 50
"race- suicide," 34
race talk, 88
racial categories, 16
racial codes, 43–44, 62, 69
racial discourse, 46
racial divide, 16
racial events, 16–17
racial formation, 29

racial inequality, 2
racialized symbolic capital, 25
racially mixed children, 34, 35, 42, 112
racial projects, 6–7
racist ideology, 34
"rainbow" families, 102
reputations of sending countries, 113
Respectful Adoption Language (RAL),
  41, *47. See also* Constructive
  Adoption Language; Positive
  Adoption Language
reverse discrimination, 16; as perceived
  by African Americans, 107–9
Roberts, Dorothy, 18

scientific model of family, 34
segregation, 17, 36; de facto, 37; de jure,
  37. *See also* Jim Crow statutes
Selman, Peter, 20
sexual orientation and adoption, 71,
  106–7
Shattered Bonds (Roberts), 18
"sincere fictions," 15
social movements, 7, 13. *See also* civil
  rights movement; women's liberation
  movement, impetus for
sources of adoption terminology, 44. *See
  also* "Adoption Glossary and
  Terminology"; *The Encyclopedia of
  Adoption*; National Adoption
  Information Clearinghouse
special needs children, 29, 42, 44, 49, 68,
  69, 71, 72, 117; adoption of by
  "second-rate" families, 117; African
  Americans as, 44; agency costs for,
  72; programs for, 49, 68, 69, 71; rates
  of adoptions of, 116; "special needs"
  as descriptor, 42; subsidization for

adoptions of, *39. See also* minority
programs; types of adoption
stereotypes of African Americans, 19, 35,
80
surveys of racial attitudes, 2
symbolic racism, 13–14

threads, 86
Toddler Adoption (Best-Hopkins), 46
transnational adoption, U.S.
    participation,: reasons for
    participation ofincreased numbers
    from sending countries, 22, 115
transnational migrants, 22
transracial adoption: 115; acceptance of,
    37; by African Americans, 40; new
    meaning of, 40; opposition by
    National Association of Black Social
    Workers, 40
tripartite system of racial categories,
    111–12
types of adoption, 8–9. *See also* adoption
    data collection; adoption programs

"unadoptable" children, 44

UNICEF, 24, 77
U.S. Department of StateState
    Department, 10. *See also* adoption
    data collection

wait time, 73
websites, 11–12; marketing, 48–49;
    search strategy, 56–59, 61. *See also*
    Internet research
"white white-habitus," 14
whiteness studies, 20
white preferences in adoption, 65, 66
white privilege, 14, 15; challenges to,
    91–92; daily effects of, 109; and
    language, 88–89, 91; and social
    networks, 14
"whitewashing," 97
Williams, Patricia, 116, 118
Winant, Howard, 6, 25
women's liberation movement, impetus
    for, 37–40; cultural and demographic
    changes, 40; impact on adoption,
    40

xenophobia, 31, 111

About the Author

Pamela Anne Quiroz is associate professor in policy studies and sociology at the University of Illinois at Chicago. She received her Ph.D. in Sociology at the University of Chicago. Her research focuses on education, inequality, identity, and children. Professor Quiroz has received research grants from the National Science Foundation, American Sociological Association, Foundation for the Scientific Study of Sexuality, and U.S. Department of Education. She has been a fellow at Stanford's Center for the Advanced Study in the Behavioral Sciences and is currently a fellow at the Institute for Research on Race and Public Policy.